Letters to my Brown Girls

Letters to my Brown Girls

4-Phases to a Liberated Life Beyond Childhood Sexual Abuse

DR. CYNTHIA SUTHERLAND

publish
your gift

LETTERS TO MY BROWN GIRLS
Copyright © 2022 Cynthia Sutherland
All rights reserved.
Published by Publish Your Gift®
An imprint of Purposely Created Publishing Group, LLC

Printed in the United States of America

ISBN: 978-1-64484-576-9 (print)
ISBN: 978-1-64484-577-6 (ebook)

Dedication

I dedicate this book to my brown girls in adult bodies who struggle with life after childhood sexual abuse.

My wish is for brown girls to have the resources they need to travel along their healing journey.

Table of Contents

Disclaimer

This publication is written for an age group of over 21 years of age. For clarity, these pages reflect actual events of inappropriate touching. These pages are meant to be read by adults.

This book references sexual abuse, depression, post-traumatic stress disorder, self-harm, and suicide. If you are experiencing suicidal thoughts or thoughts of self-harm at any time, put down this book and get help immediately. Call the National Suicide Prevention Hotline at 800-273-8255 or National Sexual Assault Hotline at 800-656-4673. This book can be used as a supplement to professional treatment and not used alone.

This book is sold with the understanding that the author is not engaged in rendering psychological, medical, or other professional medical or legal services. The author is a doctor of science in cybersecurity and education, not medical treatment. This book provides her experiences and advice as a survivor and victor only. If expert assistance or counseling is needed, the services of a licensed professional should be sought.

Introduction

To my dear brown girls,

Welcome to the beginning of your journey to heal past your traumatic experiences of childhood sexual abuse. You were strong enough to live through childhood sexual abuse. Now, here you are carving out time and space to move past the emotional and mental trauma you received from it. There is something wonderful and courageous about carving out time just for you to deal with this trauma.

I commend you for your strength and bravery. I know this wasn't easy, but I'm glad you did. Now, it's time for you to find your strength and your version of you absent of the remnants from the trauma.

You may be afraid to start your healing journey. Don't worry, you share this fear with many women and men. People fear what they don't know, and your fear is from not knowing what you may find, what you may feel or fear of who you really are. But isn't that the point of any journey, to grow as you learn?

As I grew through my healing journey, I was asked about my motivation to heal. I was asked, "Why are you addressing your childhood sexual abuse after all these years? Why now?"

Those are questions I received when family members found out about my healing journey. They were unaware that I traveled this journey for years, so they assumed that I hadn't done anything to cope or heal during *all those years.*

I responded, "Healing from childhood sexual abuse isn't something you go through. Healing is something you grow through."

Why and why now? As a teenager and young adult, it was difficult managing life through the barriers of anxiety, nighttime-fear paralysis, smiling through depression, and falsifying love to those who loved you. To feel whole and be happy, I needed to heal past those barriers. I couldn't do that when they wanted me to. I had to heal on my own time, in my own space and in my own way to find peace within myself. I knew if I wanted healthy relationships in my future, I needed to heal past my barriers of childhood sexual abuse.

What is your "why" and "why now" for taking this journey? Where do you start when deciding which path to take to heal from childhood sexual abuse? Where do you start when the path is as clear as mud? You start here.

So, find a corner, a small closet, or a spot under your favorite tree to journey down the path to break the shackles and burden of the trauma.

This journey will have bends, distractions, setbacks, and emotional challenges along the way. So, as you travel do not get discouraged. This is by design. Your objective is to focus on progression not perfection as you grow.

Writing this book was not just about providing you with a guide, companion and living proof, but also about giving you resources to help you heal. Words without actions are just words. The resources here provide actions with time and space for you to take your journey, address your barriers, and answer the below questions:

- Why heal?
- Why heal now?
- Who am I?
- Who am I after I've healed?

It is my honor to be a companion and guide on your journey as you face your fears and find comfort in the uncomfortable elements of liberating yourself from your most hurtful experiences. At this time, your path is one less traveled by many women, and you don't know what reactions and emotions you may face. However, beyond your fears and tears of the unknown is your ability to breathe and face these memories and emotions with strength and conviction. You start building strength and conviction by looking in the mirror and saying:

It doesn't matter what I find on my journey nor what my past is. Today is the day that I reset my purpose, embrace my journey and be patient with myself. Today is the day I commit to me.

Let the liberation begin.

Prologue

As I walked off the stage from my speaking engagement at an Atlanta high school, a classic-dressed male teacher greeted me with a handshake.

"Dr. Sutherland, thanks so much for sharing your story with us. I know it must've been hard speaking about being sexually abused as a child," he said.

"No, not anymore," I replied.

I grinned and proceeded to say, "If you would have asked me about the abuse in my teenage years, my response would've been anything I could do to change the subject and ignore that part of my life. In my twenties, I would've smiled on the outside, cried on the inside, then done something to make myself feel better, which more than likely was not healthy. But I've done a lot of healing to get to this point. I became happy with me, my God, my family and my career. So, I have no reserves with speaking about it."

Then he said, "I'm trying to figure out *how* is it that you are not a mental wreck? Other women I know who've been through similar situations are emotional wrecks. What did you do differently?"

This conversation is a typical conversation I've had with many people before: a sexually abused African wife in her thirties trying to escape an abusive husband, an African American teenager looking for a way out of an emotional spiral, and a Middle Eastern woman in her thirties fighting against her culture. They were curious about how I overcame the emotional and mental trauma of childhood sexual abuse plus the struggles of breaking through glass ceilings in my career as a:

- Fatherless daughter from the projects,
- Teenage mom who was a first-generation college student living on welfare,
- Two-time college dropout,
- Single mom of a black male for thirteen years,
- Army Veteran of Operation Enduring Freedom/ Operation Iraqi Freedom,
- Southern gal who left her small town for a job in the big city,
- Woman in the white male-dominated field of cybersecurity and information technology for twenty-five years,
- Doctoral student in the role of a wife, a mother, and an employee,
- Black cybersecurity professional serving as the first United States representative to a specific multinational cybersecurity board,

- Young black woman facing sexism, ageism, and racism during a seven-year climb to becoming the first senior executive service (SES) member serving as the top cybersecurity advisor for a US government agency.

This book provides my methods and timeframe used to liberate myself from the burden of trapped memories, emotions, and unhealthy habits, and be reborn into a conviction of strength and pride.

Writing this book was no easy task. I'm not a psychiatrist nor a psychologist. I had no clue how to write this book or what I wanted to put in it. All I knew was that I wanted to share resources and other information on how to heal from the curse of childhood sexual abuse with other brown women who suffered from the same trauma. During the struggle to write this book, I was approached by:

- A concerned mother who did not know *how to handle* her nine-year-old brown girl who was sexually abused.

- A male co-worker who found out his sister was being sexually abused by their father and was confused about *how to talk to her and how to help her.*

- A battered housewife during a women's retreat who told me that my story gave her *courage to start her journey* to heal from being sexually abused by her husband.

These interactions made me realize my writing had to be as vulnerable and authentic as possible to help brown women heal from the moment their trust is stolen until they heal.

As I wrote the book, I identified four stages of childhood sexual abuse: Innocence Stage is before the sexual abuse occurs, where we can be proactive with prevention and reduction of childhood sexual abuse. Stolen Trust Stage is the time when a child is left alone to defend themselves against sexual abuse with the skills they have or don't have. Critical Attention Stage is the period of time between the Stolen Trust Stage and the first year after the sexual abuse occurs. This is where the child needs delicate attention to keep them from going into themselves and creating unhealthy habits to cope with the effects of the trauma. Finally, the Surviving Stage is the time in a survivor's life where they are coping with the trauma and require help to overcome the mental and emotional barriers that built up over the years.

Letters to My Brown Girls provides a brown girl's perspective to healing from childhood sexual abuse in the Surviving Stage. The A.F.T.R. Framework is a four-phased approach for liberating survivors from unwanted and unhealthy responses to living in a new world based on new healthy habits. A.F.T.R. provides companionship, transparency, resources, and time and space for other brown girls to heal. A.F.T.R. phases are:

1. *Acknowledge* your starting point for facing your trapped memories and emotions while learning patience with yourself as you release those memories and grow through your emotions.

2. *Forgive* yourself and others as a way of releasing your emotions.

3. *Transition* to be self-sufficient in controlling yourself and accepting yourself.

4. *Rebirth* through spiritual transformation, living in your truth, and living a purposeful life to step out of the world that defined you and be born into the world that you define.

Each phase has a story, key steps, resources, and tools to address the mental and emotional barriers, successes, failures and lessons learned to help you along your healing journey. Each story, memory, etc., is offered as living proof that you are not alone in your journey to overcome childhood sexual abuse. I feel honored that you chose me as your companion.

A Readers' Guide to Using This Book

Healing from childhood sexual abuse requires more than just telling a survivor to "get over it" or "take some medication to feel better." You can't just put her in front of a psychiatrist and say, "Fix her" or in front of a pastor and say, "Pray with her." Survivors require information, resources, time, space, and practices for healing past childhood sexual abuse. This book serves as that source of information, resources, and practices.

There are self-help books written to provide women with information on surviving childhood sexual abuse. However, this book provides a brown girl's perspective on tearing down the barriers put up by the trauma of childhood sexual abuse. The chapters are structured into the below sections:

- *Purpose* provides the reason for each phase of the healing journey.

- *Memories* provides living proof that you are not alone in your experiences of childhood sexual abuse nor your healing.

- *Did You Know* connects you to information and statistics that provides different perspectives on the problem of childhood sexual abuse across America and the globe.

- *Exercises* provides steps for each phase of healing. Steps include grounding techniques, building calming environments, and moving you one step closer to your healing.

- *Experiences and Growth* provides a vulnerable approach to growth through my experience in each phase.

- *Letters to My Brown Girls* provides words of compassion, motivation, and companionship on your healing journey. These letters provide you with a voice on your journey. Additionally, letters to younger brown girls focus on empowering young brown girls to feel comfortable telling an adult if they are being sexually abused. The intent of these letters is to guide adults who struggle with words when they suspect a child is being or has been sexually abused.

- *Resources* are sources of information or activities to educate, motivate, inspire, and drive you on your healing journey. Resources for each chapter are collected at the end of the book.

Together, these sections and phases provide you with a healing journey focused on learning patience, forgiveness, self-control and self-worth. These are all elements to liberating yourself from the shackles of childhood sexual abuse. Also, if you are a(n):

1. Person who wants to understand how to help someone who experienced childhood sexual abuse or

2. Advocate looking for resources to help reduce the occurrences of childhood sexual abuse in the brown community.

I welcome you to this book and hope it gives you the resources you need on your journey to heal others.

For my brown girls, this is not an all-inclusive book, nor is it a book that guarantees success in your healing or career. That journey, my sister, is totally up to you. I can't know every scenario you will experience, but my wish is that this book is relatable to those who struggle to overcome the barriers of childhood sexual abuse that keep you from living the life you deserve.

So, as you try each exercise, grow through each emotion, and read each companion story, keep two rules at the forefront of your thoughts:

- Rule one: Have patience with yourself.
- Rule two: Healing is in the journey, not the destination.

Let's begin life A.F.T.R. childhood sexual abuse.

CHAPTER 1

Acknowledge Phase

Dear Sister Queen,

As you begin, please spend some time to take notice of what this means to you. Over the years, you've shown unbending determination to still breathe and survive. Going through life as a sexual abuse survivor strapped with hurtful childhood memories and emotions was not and is not easy. At times, those memories force their way back into your life through triggers and nightmares resulting in additional stress, anxiety, fear, and sometimes depression. Yet, here you are still breathing and surviving.

Surviving is a great achievement and a major milestone you should celebrate. Take five minutes just to appreciate that.

Now, it's time to heal past the barriers of pain, emotions, memories and survival tactics created because of the abuse you experienced as a child.

You got this book, but do you think you are ready?

Let's think about this. Do you want to: 1.) stay in your comfort zone of a cycle of anxiety, stress, anger for fear of releasing your past, or 2.) travel the path to the discomfort of the unknown, facing anxiety, stress, and anger, and building a healthy future? If you choose number one, stop reading and go back to your comfort zone. It's okay to not be ready at this time; however, you will face this decision again. I thank you for your support. However, if you choose number two, let's get at it.

Acknowledge Phase starts your healing journey. The goal on this journey is to learn what patience is, how to be patient with yourself as you experience natural reactions from your leftovers, and how to release these leftovers. It is here that you acknowledge and release your truth. Your truth is in the leftovers from the childhood sexual abuse. This effort will take about one and a half hours.

First, starting a healing journey means addressing leftovers — memories, emotions, and survival tactics — from the sexual abuse. These leftovers are representations of crimes against you. These criminal leftovers caused you to put up barriers around your physical, mental, emotional and spiritual self just to survive. However, here you are taking the first step to grow from being a survivor with the baggage of leftovers to becoming a victor with a lighter bag. So, let's lighten the load.

As your traveling companion in Phase 1, my old baggage serves as your living proof that you are not alone in your experience. For me, being sexually abused as a child occurred numerous times by multiple family members beginning around the age of three years old and ending around ten years old. To acknowledge my truth, my leftovers are shared on the following pages.

MEMORIES

Memories are powerful things. They serve as placeholders of information from life experiences. The information can be a smell, an image, or an emotion. As you experience different events, memories of these events, good and bad, are etched in your mind for recall.

Some of my favorite childhood memories are of my grandparents' farm with cows and pigs and the outhouse. Besides using the outhouse, I liked visiting my grandparents, Grandpa Claude and Grandma Azalea.

One of my favorite memories is of my grandma sitting in her chair watching my mom bathe my little, brown body in a steel tub in front of the big, black, potbelly wood-burning stove. Grandma always made sure I was clean. Laying by a fire still makes me miss her. R.I.H. Grandma Azalea.

Living with Grandma made me feel loved, but the best memories of my childhood were visiting Aunt Geraldine's house to play with my cousins. On bright sunny days, we played outside until night. At bedtime, we slept three to a single bed with two beds in a room. How I miss those days of innocent fun.

They were the happiest moments of my childhood. Then, my parents separated, and visits to my cousins became nonexistent. That was when things changed.

Moments and memories of my cousins were replaced by trauma and nightmares of sexual abuse. From three years old into adulthood, memories of my sexual abuse haunted me. The nightmares began with not just the memories, but the smell, touch, and anxiety lasted throughout my life.

Memory 1: Broken Silence

Do you remember when you were three years old? I don't remember all of it, but the moment I told my mom my secret is one I will never forget.

My mom, brothers and I lived in a poopy-green box house with cement walls and a flat roof. The house was always cold. So, some nights huddling around the kerosene heater was the only way to stay warm.

One night, while preparing for a bath, tears began to flow down my face as I stood in the bathroom. As I hesitated to get undressed, I anticipated what was coming next—washing between my legs.

When my mom entered the bathroom, she put me in the tub. As she picked up the soap and rag, muffled cries came out of my mouth. She was so deep in thought about something else that she didn't realize I was crying until she began to wash between my legs. As she looked at me, her face became smushed.

"What's wrong?" she asked.

"He puts *it* down there," I replied.

"Who is he?" she asked.

I responded, "Uncle."

She didn't reply. She just slowly dried me off, put on my night clothes, led me to bed, and told me to get in. Then she left. Tears continued to fall from my eyes until I drifted off to sleep.

After that, Uncle didn't come into my room for many nights. The poopy-green house was safe. He was gone.

Memory 2: Trusted Thief

One day, I was playing in my room when Mom walked in and said, "You're going to Aunt Snuffie's while I go to the Fly Fly."

Aunt Snuffie's house was in a neighborhood called Tank Branch. The Fly Fly was a place where adults hung out to drink and dance.

I did not like Aunt Snuffie's house[1]. Her house always smelled funny. Plus, she put stinky grass in her mouth and spit dark stuff in cups. The only good thing about going to Aunt Snuffie's house was that my cousins lived in the same neighborhood.

---

[1] For the sake of privacy, all names were changed.

When I got to Aunt Snuffie's house, I sat on the floor in front of the fire to play with my Raggedy Ann Doll.

While playing, Aunt Snuffie said, "Time for bed."

Then, she gave me bed clothes and said, "Put these on."

After putting on the clothes, I climbed onto the high bed to get comfortable under the mountain of covers. I pulled the heavy quilt back to find heavier blankets. As I nestled in, I found the best position to fall asleep.

While sleeping, a loud sound woke me. Scared to move, I peeked from under the covers to see a dark shadow standing in the doorway. As it walked closer, a familiar face appeared. The shadow was Uncle. He found me.

I lay motionless in bed thinking maybe he wouldn't find me under the mountain of blankets. The shadow walked over to my mountain and patted until it found me.

He reached for me saying, "Come out."

He pulled the covers from over my little brown body as I lay there like a doll. As he got closer, he reeked of alcohol. He continued to pull my underwear off as I cried out, "No."

He violated me.

As time went by, the visits to Aunt Snuffie's were regular and Uncle was a regular thief. Countless times, he stole pieces of me, leaving me with a fear of the night.

Memory 3: A Safe Space

One cloudy day in the fall of 1982, my mom held my hand as we walked to the doors of a big, brick building with pretty colors in the windows. We climbed the steps to two white doors that led to a green hallway decorated with pretty images on the doors and walls. As a four-year-old, the building was different than anything I had seen.

As we approached a door, it was opened by a woman with eyes and skin like mine. She smiled and said, "Come in, welcome to my class. I'm Ms. Proctor."

As we entered, I noticed the room was decorated with pretty colors, soft toys, and shapes. I thought, *I never want to leave.*

As time went by, the place became known as Head Start. Head Start became the place away where people gave me pretty things and there were other kids to play with. It was my safe space.

As I got older, memories of my broken silence, a safe space, and trusted thieves haunted my dreams for years. I did everything to not sleep alone and find safe places away from these trapped images. While on my journey to heal, bits and pieces of my memories triggered me, so I validated them through innocent conversations with family members. Diving deep into those triggers made me want to know more information about ways to heal from those horrible events and how to prevent them from happening to others.

DID YOU KNOW

Childhood sexual abuse is a horrific event that affects a child's life and future. As a child, I blamed myself for being sexually abused and carried that blame for years because I never knew the answer to these questions: Why is this happening to me? Who can help me? What is wrong with me?

Living in the South, you were told children are meant to be seen and not heard. You never questioned an adult. This was a culture of disregarding children as if they have nothing important to say. This culture resulted in me keeping my thoughts to myself. Due to my challenges, I showed signs of illiteracy that caused me to be held back in the first grade and to attend speech therapy classes.

I suffered in silence from those horrific acts because I didn't know the answers to my questions nor how to communicate. As a little girl, I wished someone would have explained what was happening to me and how I could've stopped it.

During my healing journey, information was presented to me to show how an adult or child can reduce the occurrences of childhood sexual abuse. Also, studies show that the best way to discuss serious topics with a child is to sit at their eye level when speaking to them. It removes the possibility of a child feeling intimidated. Considering this is a serious topic, have a seat. The information presented below answers key questions children may have about childhood sexual abuse:

1. What are private parts?
2. What is a minor?
3. What is age of consent?
4. What is sexual abuse?

What Are Private Parts?

Answer: Private parts are the chest, vagina, buttocks, and heart.

Children should be armed with common terms to understand what private parts are before sexual abuse occurs. It allows them to protect their private parts as well as accurately report the incident to an adult before it can happen again. When children are taught common terms — chest, vagina, buttocks, and heart, there is no confusion in the interpretation when a child is informing an adult of sexual abuse. For example: If a child is being sexually abused by someone who tells them their vagina is a cookie and a child informs an adult that Grandpa took their cookie, then the adult will never know the child is being sexually abused.

What is a Minor?

Answer: It depends on the crime and the location. A minor is not equally defined across America. From a global view, the United Nations Convention on the Rights of the Child establishes a child as a human under 18 years old (UNICEF, 2021).

Most people think that if you are under 18 you are considered a minor. That may be true for some crimes; however, when dealing with sexual abuse, the United States and each state's laws have different definitions of a minor. For example, Section 2243 of the federal law (US Code, 2022) states that the criteria of a minor is a person who:

- Has attained the age of 12 years but has not attained the age of 16 years; and,
- Is at least four years younger than the person so engaging in a sexual act; or attempts to do so.

I'm not a lawyer, so my interpretation may be off, but here it is anyway: From a federal perspective, a minor is a child under the age of 16, unless a sexual act has occurred then the term minor depends on how old the adult is.

DID YOU KNOW

Did you know that the great country of the United States consists of laws and policies not just from the federal government, but also from fifty state governments, five territories and over 574 tribal nations? (National Congress of American Indians, 2021.) The laws from each of these 630 entities can be complex and confusing.

To add to that, each state has their own definition of a minor. So, do you know your state's age for a minor?

What is Age of Consent?

Answer: It depends on the crime and the location. Did you know that the age of consent differs across the US? When it comes to sexual abuse, the phrase "age of consent" is used to identify if a child is of age to agree to have sex. Each state uses a different limit to determine age of consent. The youngest age of consent I've found is 16 years old (BHW Law Firm, 2021).

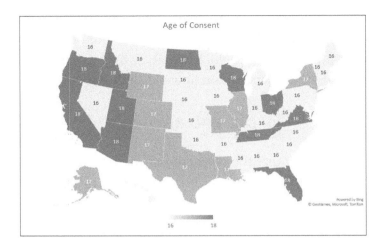

From a state level, the terms minor or *age of consent* dictate what sexual abuse is. Do you know what your state uses to determine if childhood sexual abuse has occurred?

What is Sexual Abuse?

Answer: Sexual abuse involves a *minor* in sexual activity that the minor does not understand or cannot give consent to.

These questions and answers are key pieces of information that impact defining child sexual abuse as well as investigating and prosecuting pedophiles in each state. Take the time to get to know the basic terms of your area. You may be surprised that some abusers may just walk free because of the law. Did you know that some states and countries indirectly support childhood sexual abuse by way of marriage? Child marriage is another form of childhood sexual abuse and not uncommon throughout the US. In some countries, marriage-sanctioned child sexual abuse occurs because of guardian or parental consent.

As a human being on Earth, each child has the right to protection, education, and freedom. From a global perspective, the United Nation's Universal Declaration of Human Rights and Convention on the Rights of the Child states children are entitled to be protected from sexual abuse in any country, state, city, town, street and at home (UNICEF, 2021). Any world without these rights leaves room for sexual abuse of children now and in future generations.

According to the Center for Disease Control (CDC reports, 2021), prevention and response requires people to be more aware of children's cues. Now that you know, what will you do to help a child or reduce the occurrences of childhood sexual abuse? Watch for children's cues and educate yourself on your state's laws. Awareness of the laws and rules of your environment and reporting information are major parts to saving our children from sexual abuse.

The CDC (2021) states that many kids wait to tell someone or never tell anyone about sexual abuse. When you look at the instances of child sexual abuse that are reported, the numbers show about one in every four girls and one in every thirteen boys report child sexual abuse at some point in their childhood.

The CDC (2021) states that the long-term impact of the trauma from childhood sexual abuse affects the United States economy as well. The total economic burden of child sexual abuse to the United States economy was at least $9.3 billion in 2015 (CDC, 2021). That number was based on current and past cases of child sexual abuse that were reported. Just think of what the number would be if all cases were reported.

In closing, the impact of childhood sexual abuse on a child and the neglect of it into adulthood is immeasurable. For more information about how to help younger children heal, please refer to the resources for this chapter in the Resources Section at the end of the book. As the CDC (2021) stated, childhood sexual abuse is a large community and health problem impacting the child, the economy, and the world; however, it can be prevented (CDC, 2021). The prevention and reduction of sexual abuse takes a community approach to inform and educate our children and adults. If we want to protect our children and make them feel safe, childhood sexual abuse education and awareness programs must be established in our communities. If they aren't established, it's like we are inviting other brown girls to join us in our struggle. Do you want another brown girl to suffer what you suffered from childhood sexual abuse?

As I searched for my path to healing, this information resonated with me and gave me insight and direction for developing my healing exercises; our healing exercises.

PHASE 1: ACKNOWLEDGE EXERCISE

The Acknowledge Phase is the beginning of your healing journey. The goal is to learn what patience is and how to be patient with yourself as you experience natural reactions to these trapped memories. It is here that you acknowledge and release your trapped memories and emotions of childhood sexual abuse. This effort will take about one and a half hours.

Patience is defined by Merriam-Webster Dictionary as the ability to remain calm, give attention, and wait for a long time without becoming annoyed when addressing a problem. Think about how many times you were not calm, did not give something your full attention, or didn't have time to wait to deal with a problem. How did you respond? Was it a healthy response of patience or something else? Was the problem still there afterwards? Be honest.

Trapped memories are a problem. They slither into your nightmares and thoughts to darken your mood and they can disrupt your day. To be successful in this phase, preparation for acknowledging trapped memories is key. Facing trapped memories of childhood sexual abuse causes emotions to be high.

So, you start by creating a calming, healing environment for this phase and for the remainder of your healing journey. Locate a calm, quiet space away from distractions: a place like a closet, a desk, a spot under a tree, a worship room or just a corner in your home. Then, find positive sources of energy like a plush blanket, a song, a calming aroma, an adult coloring book, a supportive friend or pet, or an open field or park. Next, collect a pen, journal lines (Appendix A), a mirror, a cup of cold water or hot relaxing tea, scissors and a timer. These materials provide you time and space to practice patience as you release your memories and emotions.

My first calming environment was a corner in my bedroom by the window with a grey, bean bag chair and a beige canopy net to hang from the ceiling. It made me feel like a butterfly in a cocoon. My positive sources of energy were my mentor, a coloring book and classical music. The differences between then and now are that my corner has an oversized chair with a table for tea, my mentor grew with me, and my classical playlist includes more brown composers.

Next, clear your mind to calm yourself from the day. You start by sitting in a comfortable position with your eyes closed. Next, slowly take five deep breaths while listening to your breath as you experience the stillness of the room. Open your eyes.

Now, take a sip of your drink. Whatever it is, close your eyes as you drink it. Think about how it feels on your tongue as it goes down. Next, take another sip, but this time don't swallow. How does it taste on the left side of your tongue compared to the right side? Now, swallow.

Next, you will identify trapped memories. To begin, set the timer for fifteen minutes. Gather your writing material (Appendix A) and start the timer. Now, write the memory of the childhood sexual abuse that has been haunting you. Even if it is unthinkable, write your memory until the timer goes off.

That previous step can bring out some serious thoughts and emotions. To calm yourself down, take five deep breaths and listen to your breath as you experience the stillness of the room. Open your eyes. Take a sip of your drink. Whatever it is, close your eyes as you drink it. Now, think about how the cup feels in your hand. Is it hot or cold? Do you need to heat it up or add more ice? If you need to heat it up or add more ice, do so.

Next, you will identify trapped emotions. Reset and start the timer for fifteen minutes to read your letter aloud to yourself. As you read the letter, write each emotion you feel in the margins of the letter. As you write the emotions, stay true to the timer.

The purpose of the timer is to keep you from going so deep into your emotions that you can't come out. If you need to repeat the above actions to bring forward additional trapped memories and their emotions, then do so. But be careful to honor the timer.

Once your memories and emotions are out, read each letter to make sure those memories and emotions are what *you* acknowledge as *your* story. Being true and authentic to your story is the only way you will be able to heal.

Once you have acknowledged all trapped memories and their emotions, calm yourself from this experience. Take five deep breaths to permit space for patience to grow as you acknowledge your truth. Now, step away from the paper for thirty minutes. During this time, use your positive source of energy to recenter yourself. This is how you learn and build patience with yourself.

You need this space to grow and learn patience because your emotions may also include the most dangerous emotion of them all—anger. Don't worry, it is normal to feel these emotions. However, you don't want to linger in them longer than needed. Dwelling on those painful memories and emotions will only cause you to become angrier. Remember to honor the timer.

If you still feel anger, the next step is to dive deep into your anger by writing a Dear John letter. Writing a Dear Anger letter (Appendix B) allows you to focus on anger by acknowledging it and wishing it farewell as if it is a lover who hurt you deeply.

Before writing this letter, think about how you met anger, what happens when you feel angry, and what you will do to it if it returns. Express every thought towards anger that you have.

Now, set the timer for fifteen minutes, start the timer, and say goodbye to anger. When the timer goes off, read the letter out loud to yourself acknowledging this as your truth.

The last step in this phase is to release the trapped memories and emotions from your life. Start by placing your letters in front of you, take three deep breaths and rip the letters down the middle from top to bottom. Then, rip across the middle from left to right. Next, cut them into little pieces with scissors until you can't read anything. Finally, destroy the remains of the paper. You can trash them, bury them, or flush them down the toilet. The key here is to release your memories and emotions including anger.

For some, these actions are good enough. For me, fire is calming. So, I placed my pieces in my fireplace and watched as the memories, emotions, and anger burned to cinders and the smoke rose to the chimney to be gone from my life forever.

Now that you've released trapped memories and emotions, please take time to appreciate your efforts. Not many people can go through pain and anger and grow in a positive way. You just did.

When I was done, I created a music playlist with my favorite songs to express my emotions and growth through this journey. These songs still hit the spot. Check out my website (www.drcys.com/blog) to find and subscribe to my Phase 1: Musical Playlist.

As we close out this exercise, understand that Phase 1: Acknowledge Phase isn't here to normalize nor undo your past, instead it is here to provide a space for you to heal. You identified and released trapped memories and emotions that were barriers to you accepting and feeling positive energy and emotions. Your baggage has been lightened my lady. Great first step.

EXPERIENCE AND GROWTH

Acts of sexual abuse were and are hard to write but doing so was necessary for me to heal. This release allowed me to break down the memories and emotions that were barriers in my life. These barriers were so deeply rooted that I didn't recognize them in my teens, twenties, or early thirties.

It was difficult to recognize these barriers because, like other brown girls in America, I had mental, emotional, and spiritual barriers from other traumatic experiences. These experiences came from living in violent neighborhoods, seeing police brutality, living in alcoholic and drug-addicted families, and racism from white and other brown people. Events like these cause barriers in your life as well, which makes the journey to heal from childhood sexual abuse a complex one.

Going through Phase 1: Acknowledge Phase, I pulled apart memories from other traumatic experiences that were piled on top of memories from the childhood sexual abuse. Separating my memories and emotions of sexual abuse from the memories and emotions of poverty and racism allowed me to focus on one traumatic experience at a time.

Experiencing the Acknowledge Phase takes courage and conviction. As I traveled this journey, acknowledging my emotions provided me time to remember that I am a human who was traumatized and that it's okay for me to feel anger. It also allowed me space to release deeply rooted anxiety, feelings of neglect, and shame. Afterwards, I was emotionally drained and needed to watch TV. So, I went to Hogwarts. The magical feeling of Hogwarts always makes me feel better.

If you need additional help, please use the resources in this chapter or lean on a friend for support. Both were very helpful for me.

LETTERS TO MY BROWN GIRLS

As you close out this phase of your healing journey and chapter in your life, think about the progress you've made over this chapter. You increased your awareness, knowledge, and self-control while also thinking about ways you can prevent and reduce childhood sexual abuse for others. If you made it this far, congratulations my brown queen. You have grown!!!!

Here and going forward, each chapter ends with letters written to close out the growth of that chapter and prepare you for the next chapter. They provide letters of encouragement for your journey.

Each letter serves a purpose. The first letter is to me from me as an example of a dialogue you can have with yourself. In addition, I must address the current problem. The second letter is from me to a younger brown girl because childhood sexual abuse is *still* a problem. These letters are for you or an advocate looking for insight on how to speak to brown girls who are experiencing childhood sexual abuse now. These letters are to be read by an adult at the child's eye level. The final letter in each chapter is my letter to you, my sister queen. These letters serve as trusted companions for your journey through your uncomfortableness.

To Me, the Little Brown Girl

Dear little brown princess,

Nice preschool graduation picture. Congratulations on graduation! Good job on getting up every day, going to school and learning! You should be so proud of yourself.

I know you were upset that you had to leave school. It was your safe space with friends and teachers but don't worry, you will find a new safe space.

How are you feeling today? I know, you feel sad most of the time. Let's talk about *why* you feel sad. If you don't want to talk. It's okay. I can wait until you are ready.

When you *are* ready, you can take your time and tell me what happens at night when Uncle comes in your room. You are a big girl, so I know you are strong enough to tell me.

If you don't feel comfortable, how about you and I talk about private parts? First, let me teach you about private parts.

Your body has what adults call private parts. Private parts are parts of your body. They are your chest that protects your heart, your buttocks that you sit on and your vagina between your legs. Boys also have a chest and buttocks, but boys don't have a vagina between their legs. They have a penis between their legs.

Every person in the world has private parts just like you. Just like everyone else's body, your body is normal. Your private parts are normal.

Someone touching or putting anything into your private parts is *not* normal. The things Uncle did to your private parts were not normal. He was wrong each time he touched your private parts and pushed his penis into your vagina. The things he did were called sexual abuse.

When you're ready, let's talk about sexual abuse. Talking to someone will make you feel better. I know you feel that no one listens to you, but you should tell your teacher or your principal about the sexual abuse you are going through. You can tell them.

Talking about what he did to you will make you feel better because once you tell someone, they will stop him from hurting you. If you tell someone and he *still* hurts you, you should tell a different person. You should keep telling someone until he stops hurting you. When he stops hurting you, the pain will stop and you will feel better.

Yes, you are scared and hurting, but I'm here to tell you that the pain between your legs will go away. Believe me, your body will heal itself and you will feel better.

It doesn't matter how small you are or the color of your skin. As a child, you should not be hurt by any adult in that way. You are beautiful and brave enough to say something to someone to stop the pain.

- Every day you wake up. Don't you? *And,*
- Every day you get out of the bed and put two feet on the floor and go. Don't you?

That means *every* day you face the world with *courage* to go through that day. One day, your courage is going to grow so much that you will write a letter to encourage other little brown girls to get up every day and try to heal. This means you shouldn't feel ashamed of what happened to you.

You are a brave little girl for just listening. Keep being brave.

Love,

Me

Little Brown Girls (brown girl under the age of 10)

To you, a pretty, brown girl,

Hi pretty girl, my name is Cynthia. This is me taking my preschool graduation picture. Yeah, I look happy. My teacher told me smiling makes me look pretty, so I smiled.

I did not want to smile because I was not feeling happy that day. I did not feel happy because a person was hurting me at night. That person hurt me by touching and hurting private parts on my body.

Private parts are what adults call parts of your body that no one else is supposed to see, touch or stick anything in. They are your chest that protects your heart, your butt on which you sit, and your vagina between your legs. Boys have private parts like you, but boys don't have a vagina between their legs. They have a penis between their legs.

To help you remember, these are parts of your body that are covered by a bathing suit.

Just in case you didn't know, your body is normal. Your private parts are normal. But when another person touches or puts anything into your private parts, this is called sexual abuse. Sexual abuse is *not* normal.

When I was the same age as you, no one told me what private parts were. No one told me that a person was not supposed to touch or insert anything into my private parts. I did not know what to do when an adult hurt me by touching my private parts.

An adult told me to be quiet and not tell anyone. So, I cried because I was hurting and scared. Secrets like this are not good because the person hurting you will just keep hurting you unless you say something.

If someone touched your private parts or if you were sexually abused, then you should tell the person reading you this letter or a family member. If you don't know how to tell them, you can use the picture of the brown girl on the next page to draw a circle on the places where you are being abused. Then you can give the drawing to them or someone you trust. If you don't trust the person reading you this letter, tell someone else.

Either way, it is totally up to you who you tell and how you tell them. I don't crae what you do as long as you tell someone.

You're supposed to be safe from harm and the pain of someone hurting your private parts. One day you will be safe, but it's up to you.

Be brave enough to speak to someone to stop the pain. Know that I believe in you. You can do this.

Love,

Cynthia

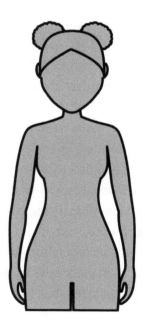

Brown Girls (25 and over)

My Dear Sister Queen,

WOW! What a journey. You've made it through the first phase, the Acknowledge Phase. Yeah, you had to face trapped memories and emotions, but most importantly, you learned how to wait on yourself — your thoughts, your emotions, and your growth. That was patience.

I know reading this chapter was a challenge. Living it was also a challenge, but writing it was necessary.

Releasing memories through writing allowed me to deal with the memories that haunted me for years and gain clarity in my emotions. As I wrote my experiences, bottled up emotions from my childhood came out along with other emotions I didn't know even existed. Sometimes memories came with a single emotion. At other times, emotions flooded every being of my body at once. Dealing with a single emotion was easy; however, the flood of emotions was where I practiced the most patience with myself. Growing through my emotions were my most freeing moments.

So, I ask that you accept your journey and growth during this phase and chapter in your life. Not to overanalyze the journey and growth, but to admit the past happened and cannot be changed. Now, you move forward to focus your energy on your continued growth in the next phase.

Your next and final step in this healing phase is to write your letter to yourself (Appendix C) at the age you were sexually abused. Comfort yourself, and most importantly, show compassion for yourself. Once you are done, put it in a sealed envelope within your favorite book. This will be used as the baseline of your thoughts for the next three phases.

I wish you enlightenment and growth as you close out this chapter of your journey. See you in the next phase.

Love,

Cynthia

Resources

Resources for this chapter are provided to address the prevention of childhood sexual abuse, reduction of the occurrence of child sexual abuse, and for healing and coping in private and public. Due to the special nature of this chapter, these resources also provide immediate help for children you may know who are currently being sexually abused.

Please refer to the end of the book for resources and my website (www.hidntrezher.org) for updated resources.

CHAPTER 2

Forgive Phase

Dear Sister Queen,
The Acknowledge Phase was a hard one to get through. Your greatest accomplishment in that phase was learning how to have patience with yourself while growing through your emotions. This growth allowed you to rip down emotional barriers holding you back from healing.

Next, we look at one of the key efforts to healing from childhood sexual abuse—forgiveness. For some sexual abuse survivors, forgiveness is the last thing they want to think about. I ask that you have an open mind as you read about what forgiveness is not, what it is, its benefits, and what you can do to forgive. I must forewarn you of two misconceptions about forgiveness. Forgiving is not forgetting. Forgetting means overlooking what someone did to harm you. When you overlook harmful actions of a person, you leave yourself vulnerable for it to happen again. So, no, you do not forget. Learn from the "how" so that you can prevent childhood sexual abuse from happening again to someone else.

Also, forgiving is not reconciling. Reconciling means to restore balance between two parties. Balance cannot be created in childhood sexual abuse because there is no equality between a child's mental state and an adult's mental state. These are two different mental levels.

In Phase 2: Forgive Phase, you acknowledge the decision to forgive, learn how to forgive, then you forgive those whose actions resulted in you being sexually abused as a child. The goal is to see why forgiveness is key in healing from childhood sexual abuse. In its simplest form, forgiving someone consists of two elements: a decision and an action. The *decision* is to identify whether you want to deal with the emotions of fear and anger towards a person or not. The *action* is to face, overcome, and release that fear and anger towards that person, even if it is you whom you must forgive.

As you think about forgiveness, how do you determine who you should forgive for their role in your childhood sexual abuse? To gain your peace, what person will you liberate from the shackles of your mind?

Growing through my emotions in the Acknowledge Phase helped me uncover harbored anger and blame towards not just the pedophiles, but my parents and even myself. On my healing journey, I found this quote from an anonymous person: "Forgive others not because they deserve forgiveness, but because you deserve peace." This was a strong statement. I thought, *Why not try forgiveness?* I wanted peace of mind and peace in my heart.

So, I decided to start the journey to forgive my abusers, my parents and myself. To guide you in determining who you should forgive, I share with you my thoughts, my emotions and my journey to forgive.

MEMORIES

Four generations of my family grew up on Tank Branch, a neighborhood within the small, predominately white, country town of Gaffney, South Carolina. In the eighties, Tank Branch was a very poor neighborhood with a one-mile radius beginning at the Tank and never crossing the railroad tracks to the east.

Tank Branch consisted of the hood and the projects. There was a clear distinction between the hood and the projects in the eighties, but then the crack epidemic blurred the line between the hood and the projects.

Tank Branch molded me for eight years. Like the rest of poor, black America in the eighties and nineties, I experienced my share of:

- Injuring my wrist from cutting thick blocks of government cheese.

- Spending brown and purple food stamps.

- Watching violent street fights between adults over a man or some gossip.
- Winos urinating in the street.
- Crack heads creeping in the dark.
- Generational curses of alcoholism and domestic violence.

These are the events of my habitat that shaped my habits. These moments in time shaped my ability to trust, my anxiety, my fear and my anger. Memories and moments on Tank Branch created who you see today.

Memory 4: The Hood

At seven years old, my mom, my two brothers, and I moved to a house in the hood on Tank Branch. The house belonged to a big momma who lived above us. We lived under the stairs in a dark, damp, basement in a big, creepy house along with an aunt and her three sons.

As a child in the house, my mom warned me to limit my time upstairs or else I would anger the big momma. To avoid angering her, I tried my best to stay in the basement or outside.

On days after school, I went outside to play with my cousins. We played games like hide and seek; red light, green light; and Red Rover. Outside was safe.

When inside, I could not talk nor laugh. So, I played with my She-Ra doll and castle in the basement. She-Ra was my best friend. She had a sword and a shield. She could fly away on her Pegasus, Swift Wind, whenever she wanted to. Plus, she lived by herself in her own castle. Oh, what a great life She-Ra had.

Moving to Tank Branch also meant I had to start a new elementary school. Except for having to repeat the first grade, the new school was ok. At seven years old, I couldn't read nor speak well, so I went to speech therapy and reading comprehension class in addition to my regular class. The class was fun because I was introduced to my first computer, the Apple II, which taught me how to read using games like The Oregon Trail.

Even after a couple of months, school was still better than the big momma's house. Besides being bullied and called names like "nigger," "jap" and "chinq," it was better than home. The new school became my safe place.

Weekdays were good, but weekends were still the same. The move to Tank Branch put us two minutes away from Aunt Snuffie's. During the weekends, my mom continued to take me to Aunt Snuffie's house before leaving for the Fly Fly, the Carolina Club, and wherever else adults went to drink, smoke and dance. I hated going to Aunt Snuffie's because sometimes Uncle would show up to steal from me at night.

As time went by, my life was what it was...normal. In this normal life, I wished to be taken away from the pain. But no one came to take me away. But who could take me away? I didn't know anyone.

One day, I was playing in the basement when my mom called me from upstairs.

She yelled, "Come upstairs."

As I emerged from the basement, she said, "Come, look out the window, it's your daddy."

I walked over to look out the living room window.

There was a stranger in a car in front of the big momma's house. That stranger didn't look like my daddy. I gave my mom a confused look.

She looked at me and said, "That's your real daddy."

I didn't know the difference between a "daddy" and a "real daddy," and I was too scared to ask.

She took me outside to meet this "real daddy." This man did not look anything like my daddy. I knew my daddy and that was not him. The stranger sat in the car with a little girl in the backseat. My mom and the "real daddy" began to talk. As they talked, I got distracted by a box in his lap.

He handed me the box and said, "I hope you like it."

I accepted the box and stood there quietly as the adults talked. I don't remember anything they said.

When the adults stopped talking, I ran around the house into the basement, excited to see what was in the box.

I opened the present to see a pretty, pink box with the name of the doll on the front. I opened the box to see a new doll with clothes and a brush and … and … and that was it.

The doll didn't have anything but clothes. I thought to myself, *This doll is not like She-Ra. She doesn't have anything to protect herself. She-Ra has a sword and shield. She-Ra is a hero, a protector and unlike ANY person I have ever met. This doll has nothing, not even a horse with wings to take her away. She's just a simple doll with clothes.*

She-Ra was my best friend. I didn't like living in the big momma's damp, dingy, stinky basement, but having She-Ra made it better. She-Ra was the only person who loved me. She-Ra was there when I needed her. As time went by, I accepted that no one was going to fly me away, but at least I had She-Ra.

Memory 5: Moving on Up to the Projects

One day in 1986, my mom said, "We are moving out of the basement."

I thought to myself, *No more basement; no more stinky clothes; no more rushing water in scary, leaky pipes; and most important of all, no more wading through flooded floors.*

Then, on a beautiful, sunny day, a car and truck pulled up beside the big momma's house to collect our furniture. I watched as my mom's boyfriend and others packed up the beds and the couch onto the truck. With all the commotion, I grabbed She-Ra and Swift Wind to leave. I jumped into the car and left the big momma's house with my mom and brothers and never, ever, ever wanted to live there again.

I was so excited to move to the projects. When the car pulled up in front of the building, I jumped out of the car to follow my mom down the small hill and up the concrete sidewalk to the white, metal door with a small, black, wooden sign beside the door showing the apartment number.

I entered the sunlit apartment and immediately felt the cleanliness and warmth of living in the projects.

As I stood in the living room, my mom said, "You have your own room."

She walked me down the hall to my very own room. I was so happy as I walked through the door into a pretty, white room with cement walls and a hard, white, dry, clean floor. The bedroom window had a white rollup shade drawn halfway so the beautiful sun could shine in. I loved my new room.

With excitement, I ran around the apartment exploring each room. The kitchen was bright with a stove that made clicking sounds when you turned it on. The bathroom was white, clean, and had a toilet with a lid. There were windows in every room. Most important of all, the front and back doors had big locks and metal screen doors that locked. I leaped with excitement. The projects was home.

Memory 6: The Bus Stop

Soon after moving into the projects, I started second grade. On the first day of school, I was nervous about waiting at the bus stop. The only person I knew in the projects was my mom's boyfriend. He was from the projects, so, he knew how everything worked.

Normally, my mom's boyfriend didn't speak to me much.

That day, he saw I was nervous and said, "I'll walk you to the bus stop."

He took my hand and we left for the bus stop.

As we walked up the long sidewalk, the sounds of children playing, buses going by and cars honking horns made me nervous. There was lots of movement, yelling, running, playing and laughing. I had never seen so many kids at a bus stop.

The bus stop's center of attention was a brick wall. Kids from high school and elementary gathered around the wall to wait for the bus. The wall had metal letters which the bigger boys used as steps for climbing the wall. They sat on the wall looking down on us as we all waited on the bus.

Once there, my mom's boyfriend waited with me until the bus pulled up.

Before letting go of my hand, he looked at me and said, "You gone be ok."

From then on, I liked my mom's boyfriend, Dan.

As the days went by, Dan stopped walking me to the bus stop. From then on out, my journey to the bus stop was a lonely one. My nerves kept me from getting too close to the wall. My distance was far enough to see what was going on, but close enough to walk to the bus when it pulled up. As I stood watching, I prayed other kids wouldn't talk to me, while also wanting a friend. So, I kept my head down.

Memory 7: Another Trusted Thief

WARNING – THE FOLLOWING CONTENT MAY BE UPSETTING TO SOME INDIVIDUALS

Moving to the projects resulted in less visits to Aunt Snuffie's and the big momma's house and less visits from Uncle. I loved living in the projects. It was my new safe home. At least, until...

One night, my mom and Dan went out leaving another uncle to babysit us. As the night went on, we watched TV until bedtime. Even though I had my own room, I still slept in my little brothers' room. As we entered the room, they fell out in the bottom bunk and I climbed to the top bunk, crawled under the covers and went to sleep.

Time passed as I slept. After some time, I was awakened by the slow creak of the door opening. As my eyes focused, a shadow stood in the doorway looking into the room. Immediately, fear paralyzed me.

As the shadow turned around to leave, the bathroom light revealed the shadow man as Uncle #2. Then, the door closed behind him. I took a deep breath and laid there struggling to go back to sleep.

Then, the door opened again, but this time it swiftly closed with Uncle #2 standing in the room. As the shadow got closer, fear paralysis consumed me again. He walked to the side of the top bunk and began searching for my body. Tears built up as he pulled my legs apart with his strong hands. My body wasn't strong enough to keep my legs closed.

As he pushed my panties to the side, I whimpered, "No, please stop."

Then, his fingers assaulted me as I cried. Finally, he stopped, turned around and left. I shrunk into my covers and cried myself to sleep. The projects was not safe anymore.

The next morning, I woke with fear of his return. I knew he would come back and do it again. Where can I go? I thought, *I will run away. Yes, run away, but to where?*

The woods. But the woods have animals, insects and leaves of poison ivy. There is no other option. I had to choose.

I chose to live in the woods. So, I grabbed my teddy, put on my shoes, and ran out the back door of the apartment down the steps, under the clotheslines full of clothes, then through the backyard, down the asphalt hill and across the parking lot to hide behind two dark green dumpsters.

I peeped around the dumpsters to see if anyone was looking. When it was clear, I sprinted into the forest through the tall weeds and over vines and broken tree limbs. After running for what seemed like forever, I turned around and saw no one. I was free in the woods.

The forest was quiet and safe. I walked through the trees thinking, *This isn't too bad. I can do this.*

After walking for some time, I came upon a tall, metal, chain link fence stretching towards the sky. Halfway up the fence was a sign that read, "No Trespassing." I thought, *I've never seen a fence that high before. Something dangerous must be on the other side. Plus, I've never climbed a fence that high before.* So, I sat on the ground, looked up at the sky and thought, *What am I gonna do? I don't wanna go back. I'm tired of being hurt. I can't stay home.* So, I laid on the forest floor and cried.

As I laid there crying, insects began crawling around me—a black centipede, a green stick bug and other bugs with ugly legs and scary markings. I jumped up and dusted the bugs off me. I thought, *I can't live in the woods with bugs at night, but I have nowhere else to go.* I had to make a choice: live in the woods with bugs that could kill me at night, climb the fence to something that might kill me or go back home. So, I stood up and went home.

Memory 8: My First Friend

As time went by, I accepted my new normal life and went about my days. On the weekdays, I went to the bus stop with the rest of the Project kids. On the weekends, I prayed my mom would stay home or that someone else would babysit us instead of Uncle #2.

One day in third grade, a classmate named Tisha asked me if I wanted to come to her house to play. I could not believe that someone asked me over to their house to play.

Tisha said, "I could meet you at the bus stop."

"What bus stop?" I asked.

She replied, "By the wall where we get on the bus in the mornings and then I can walk you to my house."

I never saw Tisha at the bus stop before. I never even knew a girl my age lived in the projects.

After school, I rode the bus home excited to play with a new friend. When we got off the bus, Tisha escorted me to her apartment. I could not believe what I saw. Tisha lived in the building right behind mine. I could see my back door from her apartment. Our apartments were separated by the clotheslines and a tree.

On weekdays, Tisha showed me lots of new things like how to play, how to make mud pies and where the park was. The monkey bars, the metal slide and the swings were fun, but Tisha's favorite was the merry-go-round. We took turns pushing each other. The smell and spinning of the metal wheel always made me want to vomit, but Tisha liked it. She became my best friend.

I feared the weekends. I never knew if my mom and Dan were going to leave us with Uncle #2 or someone else. To avoid Uncle #2, I stayed at Tisha's house as much as possible. Her house felt safe. Even though her little brother got on my nerves, her mom and dad were nice and funny. I did anything to stay with her, even lie to her mom and my mom.

On weekend nights when my mom said Uncle #2 would babysit, I told her I was staying with Tisha even if I wasn't. As much as Tisha and I asked, her mom would not let me stay as often as I wanted to. So, on nights when I couldn't stay with her, I left out the back door before Uncle #2 came, took clothes from the clothesline and slept on the ground between our apartment building and the forest. I was safer there.

Memory 9: Safe Houses

Growing up, we had a roulette wheel of babysitters: sitters who were safe, sitters who were mean, sitters who had older brothers that touched my private parts, and sitters who tickled me so hard milk would come out my nose. However, after some time, I became old enough to babysit my siblings. I saw this an opportunity for me to be free. I began to beg my mom to let me babysit. I reminded her that I was ten years old, knew the rules and I did not need a babysitter. I knew the rules:

- Do not answer the door for anyone.
- Do not burn her house down.
- Do not jump on the furniture.

- Do not touch the VCR or record player.
- Do not, most importantly, go in her room.

After much begging, my mom agreed I was big enough to babysit my youngest brother when my other siblings left. My insides were happy. I thought, *Yes!!! No more uncles.*

When it came time for me to babysit, I locked the back screen door, the big locks on both doors and all the windows. I turned off all the lights in the house. Then my brother and I watched TV and played with toys until we went to sleep. We were safe. I was safe.

Word got out that I was old enough to babysit. One day, Maggie, Dan's cousin, asked Momma if I could babysit for her. Maggie said she would pay me to stay at her house and watch her little girl, so Momma agreed.

Maggie's apartment was two rows and one block behind ours. When I got to Maggie's apartment, she showed me the prettiest baby doll I ever saw. She had yellow skin, chubby cheeks, a pretty smile, and lots of hair. It was love at first sight. All I wanted to do was protect and love her. She was perfect.

Maggie taught me how to fix her bottles, change her diapers and feed her. She only cried when she was hungry, so I always made sure she had food. After a couple of times babysitting, I never wanted to go home. I stayed with Maggie as much as possible, even when I wasn't babysitting. She bought my favorite cereal and made me scrambled eggs and grits with lots of butter. Maggie's fried liver mush and bologna always had crispy edges. Her apartment felt safe.

As time went by, word traveled around the projects that I was a good babysitter. More people started to request my babysitting services. For the next six years, I babysat Tina, Jessica, Joanie, Lil Tony, Tay, Lil Terry, Misha, Red, the twins, and at least twenty-nine other kids—ranging from newborns to eleven years old—from eighteen different families. My eighteen safehouses allowed me to sleep in comfort, eat what I wanted and watch what I wanted. Those families kept me away from pain, fear, anxiety and anger.

My life in the hood and the projects shaped me for the good and the bad. However, the many strong, brown women who hired me saved me from additional victimization. They became my guardians.

DID YOU KNOW

The journey to healing as a childhood sexual abuse survivor is not easy. As a child, many questions run across your mind like, "Why me? What did I do wrong?" When you talk to your close friends they say, "Oh, it wasn't your fault. You were just a child. You couldn't have done anything to stop it." I understood that a person is supposed to say that to you, but something in you still yearns for answers.

Did you know that after World War II, criminal theorists identified the Routine Activities Theory (RAT) as a framework to understand why crime increased across America? RAT states that a crime occurs with the combination of four elements: 1.) a vulnerable target, 2.) motivated offender with capabilities, 3.) lack of a capable guardian to protect the vulnerable target and 4.) availability of time and space (Oludare, 2015). When you apply RAT to childhood sexual abuse, it occurs when a motivated offender (a sexual predator) identifies a vulnerable target (a child) without a capable guardian (a parent or older family member) in a space with available time (home alone). Understanding these factors helps you answer your questions plus identify which element you want to change to reduce and prevent the occurrence of childhood sexual abuse.

So, I dove deep into the crime of childhood sexual abuse and applied RAT to understand *why* it was *not* my fault. For example, as a child, you cannot control your vulnerability of being smaller and weaker than an adult criminal.

Also, the lack of a capable guardian is also not on you. A guardian guards you, but they also must have the capabilities to defend you against the criminal. Your guardian must be just as strong or stronger or just as smart or smarter than the pedophile. You cannot control someone's responsibility to guard you nor their capabilities to defend you.

Additionally, you cannot control the motivations of a criminal. A pedophile's motivation is sex with a child. Sex is what motivates them. You cannot control their motivation.

Finally, your home provides you space and time, but it also belongs to others. Did you know that 91% of child sexual abusers are someone the child or family knows? (CDC, 2021). As a child, you cannot control who comes into a space you occupy, and you cannot control the relationships of your family.

Child Sexual Abuse

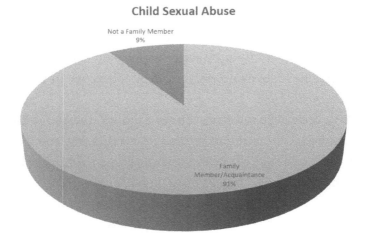

Understanding these factors helped me see why childhood sexual abuse was not my fault. The motivation of pedophiles is disturbing, but there is nothing you can do about someone else's motivation. It's not your issue to address.

There's something wrong with them. They are the ones that need help to control their urges. So, walk away from any thoughts about why it happened to you and what you did wrong. You did nothing but live.

As I was having a conversation with a friend about the book, she revealed she was unaware of my culture. Then she asked about the differences between poverty, being poor, a hood, and the projects. In summary, I told her:

- Poverty is living without enough money to feed a family of two or more, in a four-bedroom home with three different families of 11 people, roaches and rodents. Poor is a single family of three or more living in a three-bedroom, rent-controlled apartment with food from the Women, Infants, and Children (WIC) program, paper food stamps and just enough money from a low-paying job to buy necessities. Memories of watching wrestling, "G.I. Joe," "ThunderCats," "She-Ra," and "Transformers" and eating King Kong Vitamins, government cheese, sugar water and sugar toast bring back feelings of poverty that I wouldn't trade for the world.

- Some want to sum the hood and the projects up in one word: ghetto. But those from the ghetto know the difference. The hood is your neighbor-*hood* of houses where you grew up. Generations of families live in houses on the same street or in the same house. In my hood, most of the houses were rented while only a few families were blessed to own their home. The projects belong to the city, the county, or a slum lord and house multiple families. No one owns an apartment. For those who are calculating, property ownership is the difference. But the constants in both the hood and the projects are lack of resources to improve the way of life and the presence of juke joints, corner stores, liquor stores, small churches, funeral homes and limited tax money going into the community from homeownership.

As a little girl, I didn't understand what was really happening in my environment. Based on criminal theories, these factors were stacked against me and increased my risk of being sexually abused. However, these factors didn't determine my destiny.

Breaking down the crime of childhood sexual abuse identifies factors we, as a community, can target to prevent and reduce occurrences of childhood sexual abuse. Now that we know the factors, we can help others understand them for prevention, detection, and reduction of childhood sexual abuse.

PHASE 2: FORGIVE EXERCISE

In the last chapter, you acknowledged and dismissed anger towards the memories and the overall trauma. In this chapter, you acknowledge anger towards those people involved in your abuse and release that anger. In Phase 2: Forgive Phase, you acknowledge the decision to forgive, learn how to forgive then you forgive those whose actions resulted in you being sexually abused as a child. The goal is to see why forgiveness is key in healing from childhood sexual abuse.

From the moment you were sexually abused, negative emotions entered your body. Emotions such as fear, anxiety and anger are common for a child after being sexually abused. If these emotions aren't addressed, a child can grow up with these negative emotions in the backdrop of their life. As they get older, these emotions become ingrained into their life as moods and insecurities that keep them in bondage. This bondage can result in depression, unhealthy relationships and unhealthy habits.

If you are still in bondage due to these negative emotions, insecurities and unhealthy habits, it's time for you to forgive. To liberate yourself from this bondage of negativity, you must first acknowledge if negative emotions exist towards that person.

Looking back at the pedophile or your guardian, do you feel any anger towards them in their role of your sexual abuse? Ask yourself, "Do I still feel fear or anger towards them?" Whether it is anger towards your guardians for not being capable or present or the pedophile who exploited your vulnerabilities, you must acknowledge if the fear and anger still exist.

If it doesn't, congratulations. You can move to the next section. If these negative emotions exist, the next step is to acknowledge the requirement to release it as a part of the healing journey. Do you think releasing anger, fear, or anxiety is necessary to heal? Yes or no? Do you want to allow any of these emotions to keep you trapped in the past? Yes or no?

Yeah, people are always saying, "Forgiveness is for you, not them," but what does that mean? It doesn't mean what the abuser did to you isn't the worst act imaginable done to a child, because it was. What they are saying is that when you forgive, you release years of anger from your mind, body and spirit. Think about it. These negative emotions keep your inner peace hostage. Do you want peace?

When you're ready to forgive, you must make the decision. The decision to forgive is yours alone. When you are ready, make the decision to take the next step to release that anger, fear, and anxiety.

In the next step, you will perform the action of forgiving. You will ground yourself to face your emotions then release your fear and anxiety by writing letters to yourself, your abuser and anger. This effort will take at least one and a half hours and writing material (Appendix D), your mirror, another cup of cold water or hot tea, scissors, an Internet connection, speakers/headphones, and your timer.

You start by going to your calming environment that you created in Phase 1. Then, collect your favorite positive sources of energy from the last phase or try something different like meditation music or visit my website to catch the latest positive source or playlist.

Next, take the next five minutes to clear your mind. You start by sitting in a comfortable position with your eyes closed. Next, slowly take five deep breaths while listening to your breath as you experience the stillness of the room. Open your eyes. Now, take a sip of your drink. Think about how it feels on your tongue as it goes down. Next, take another sip, but this time don't swallow. How does it taste on the left side of your tongue compared to the right side? Now, swallow.

We start with forgiving the most important person on this journey...you. Forgive yourself for how you treated yourself over the years. Were you nice to your mind, body and spirit or did you abuse it because of anger and residual negativity from the sexual abuse? Start by pulling out your journal lines (Appendix D) and a pen and set the timer to 30 minutes. Now start the timer and write:

Sexual abuse was not my fault. I was a child.
Fear, anger and anxiety will no longer control my life.
I am stronger now.
I forgive me.

Gaze at what you wrote. Now, repeat those sentences slowly three times in the mirror to allow yourself to feel emotions. If you feel like you want to cry, cry. If you want to stomp, then stomp. The best thing you can do for yourself at this point is feel. Do this until your timer goes off. Respect the timer.

Now, take fifteen minutes to connect with your positive source of energy: green grass to feel life, relaxing music to feel the emotions of the rhythm, a prayer closet to feel the presence of your higher power or calling or a person with a positive vibe that makes you smile.

Next, you are going to write a letter to the abuser or anyone who was involved in your sexual abuse. The letter (Appendix E) is a dialogue with the person where you express your anger regarding their role and actions in your sexual abuse.

Set and start your timer for thirty minutes. Begin writing every thought that crosses your mind and every emotion you feel in your body. But when the timer goes off, *stop* writing. You must stop writing here. Remember: honor the timer.

Next, reset the timer for five minutes. Stand up, start the timer, and walk away from the letter. Retreat to your positive source of energy.

The last step in this phase is to release your anger. You start by placing all of your letters from this exercise in front of you. Inhale enough air to fill your lungs and your stomach. Do this three times. Now, rip the letters down the middle from top to bottom then across the middle from left to right. Next, cut them into little pieces with scissors. If you feel you need to do something more than cutting, ripping or shredding, then make it a burning ceremony to free your emotions and thoughts of this person.

Finally, face the mirror and say, "I forgive you, (<u>name of the person</u>). I no longer feel anger towards you. I accept you for who you are."

The best part about this activity is that you don't have to tell anyone about your forgiveness. Not even the abuser. This is for you, not anyone else.

Now, you've forgiven acts of childhood sexual abuse against you. You've released the negative energy from your life. Don't go back to it. Don't lean on it. Don't let your environment or your habits take you back to mistreating your mind, body or soul. That is not who you are anymore. You are in a different place now. To recenter yourself, refer to the Chapter 2 Resources at the end of the book.

EXPERIENCE AND GROWTH

This phase was the hardest but most rewarding phase for me. My experience with forgiveness was one of enlightenment and gaining greater perspective on life and humanity. Before my journey in Phase 2: Forgiving Phase, my faith in God was the size of a mustard seed. However, after this phase, my faith in God and myself grew stronger because He showed me signs, I listened, and the results were phenomenal.

My first sign was provided on the night of Super Bowl Sunday 2014. I was visiting family in Gaffney. The plan was to rest at Maggie's house before heading back home to D.C. at 5:00 a.m.

As I was leaving my grandma's house, my friend, Josie, asked me to take a guy home because she didn't want to drink and drive. I hesitated to respond because the guy freaked me out. He was an old wino, but she knew him. Plus, I didn't want her drinking and driving. So, I agreed to take him home.

After pulling up to Josie's in my SUV, she came outside to tell me where he lived. He got into the passenger side as the stench of alcohol flooded my truck. As he talked, the smell got worse.

We were driving along and as I made a right turn towards his house, he said "No, go left."

I said, "No, I know where you live. We aren't making any detours. I'm driving straight to your house."

As I drove on, he started rocking back and forth in his seat like a psycho. He repeatedly sung a song, "I'm in the car with Cynt."

That creeped me out. I prayed, *Lord, get me there quick.*

Once we approached his house, he said, "Thank you for brangin' me home. Can I kiss you?"

I said, "What the hell?! No."

When I pulled up into his yard, he came across my armrest to kiss me anyway. I pushed him away as he continued to try to touch me. I punched him in the face and yelled, "Get the fuck out of my car. I don't like you."

He sat back in the passenger seat and said, "I'm sorry. I'm sorry."

He quickly got out of my car. I put my car in reverse and left.

As I drove to the projects, my hands were trembling with fear. All I wanted to do was leave and go home, but I knew I needed sleep to make that seven hour drive home. Then, I got a call from my mom asking me to pick up my older cousin, Rob, from a Super Bowl party to take him home because she had been drinking and didn't want to drive. I was tired, but I wanted everyone to be home safely. So, I agreed.

I drove to the house where Rob was. When I pulled up, he got into the car smelling like alcohol and immediately began making jokes. After what I had just been through, boy did I need that laugh. He just kept making jokes and laughing. He was soooo drunk.

As I was driving, he started talking about random stuff. Then he looked at me and said, "We had fun when we were little. Didn't we?"

"Yeah, I guess so," I responded.

"Do you remember when we used to play together?" he asked.

I replied, "No, but then again, I do remember you shooting your sister from your feet like a cannon ball."

He looked at me and said, "Oh, you don't remember how I used to play with you and kiss on you?"

I looked at him confused and asked, "What are you talking about? I don't remember playing with you like *that*."

As I pulled into the parking lot he said, "I used to touch your p***y and I wonder if we can do that again?"

I fell back in my chair with disgust. I couldn't believe he said that.

"I can't believe you. That is damn disgusting," I yelled.

He sat there looking at me and smiled as if nothing was wrong. I looked at him and said, "If you don't get the fuck away from me, I'm going to hurt you."

He got out of my car and went into his apartment.

I sat there in shock. I couldn't believe he said that to me. After a night like that I thought, *If I don't leave now, I'm going to kill someone.* To save myself, I immediately left for D.C. at 1:00 a.m. I drove six hours straight only stopping once for gas. When I returned home, I didn't speak to anyone. My husband asked if I was okay. It took weeks before I could even explain what happened to me.

Those interactions didn't just happen. Why would the Universe send me through those experiences? What was

God trying to tell me? The only answer I could come up with was that those were signs that I needed to continue my healing journey to forgiveness. In my response to this enlightenment, I knew I was on the right path, but I was so scared of what I might find on the path. However, I knew I had to continue.

So, I went through the steps to release my anger and forgive those who harmed me. I wrote my letter to anger, my abusers and my parents. However, I wanted to correct and strengthen my relationships with my parents and my family. So, I attempted reconciliation with my parents and Uncle #2.

My attempts at reconciliation were done using two separate processes: Carefrontation and Confrontation. A Carefrontation is when you approach those you care about with an issue that bothers you with the intent of healing the relationship. Confrontation is when you approach someone who harmed you with the intent of clarifying the harm and creating balance in your thoughts. Both are best done when you are with that individual at a *safe* time and in a *safe* space with a capable guardian in reach and no distractions from your intentions.

Forgive Myself

In my forgiveness letter to myself, I acknowledged my role in my sexual abuse as an uninformed, uneducated, vulnerable target. I was not aware of what private parts were nor the value of private parts to adults, nor what to do when someone touched them. Because of this, I should not blame myself.

On my journey, I realized I had treated myself dirty throughout my teenage and young adult years. I was not fair to myself and needed to treat myself better. So, I wrote: Sexual abuse was not my fault. I was a child. It will no longer control my life. I am stronger now. I forgive me.

I forgave myself for my actions, my thoughts and most of all my emotions for the last 30 years. Then, I asked God for His forgiveness.

Forgive My Abusers

As I continued my healing journey, I found a series of soul healing TV shows on my favorite network owned by a black woman. One night, I fell asleep on my bedroom couch watching a TV show about the impact of a father not being in a girl's life. The next morning, while dressing for work, I turned the TV back on. As I was dressing, I heard the familiar voice of a doctor speaking to a guy about his time in prison as a pedophile. Interesting right?

I started to watch the TV. Long story short, a pedophile in California was being interviewed about his healing journey in front of a live studio audience of parents. The pedophile informed the doctor that when pedophiles are supposedly going to treatment to be "cured" or "fixed," they are taught to control the urges of wanting sex from a child. He also said that pedophile's urges for a child are the same urges a man gets for a woman or a woman gets for a man.

At that *very* moment, my heart dropped because I know how I feel when I see a man with broad shoulders, a chiseled back, a nice smile, a strong face and other nice assets. I know that I will always feel that way about a man, which made me think that a pedophile's feelings are strong and never go away.

This enlightenment made me think about those that abused me. I knew my abusers' locations. Uncle died in a freak accident after getting high on crack. Rob was homeless roaming Gaffney in an alcoholic daze. Uncle #2 lived alone as a functioning crack addict.

So, on July 3, 2014, I caught a flight to South Carolina to jump deeper into my Forgive Phase. I informed two close family members of my whereabouts and what my intentions were while there. They gave me mental and emotional support as I traveled my journey.

When I landed, I went straight to Uncle #2's house where he lived alone. As I drove up to the house, I noticed his girlfriend's car was at her house next door. Everyone knows she watches his house like a hawk, so I knew she would be over soon enough. So, I was safe.

After getting out of the car, I politely asked him if we could speak inside of the house. As we walked through the kitchen door, I stayed by the door as he walked into the kitchen.

I said, "Hey, I want to talk to you about something."

He looked at me and turned towards the cabinet to grab his weed.

As he began rolling a blunt, I asked, "Do you remembered what you did to me?"

As he held his head down, he replied, "I don't know what you are talking about."

"When I was little, living in the projects and you babysat us, you molested me," I specified.

He repeated himself, "I don't know what you talkin' about. Plus, why you brangin' all this stuff up after all these years?"

I patiently replied, "Because you hurt me. You stole from me. And despite your selfish ways of taking from me, a child, I still came out stronger on the other side."

He said, "I don't know what you talkin' about."

I said, "Thank you for giving me this time, but I want you to know that I remember what you did, and I forgive you."

He replied, "What?"

I said it again, "I'm no longer angry with you. I forgive you."

Before he could say anything else, his girlfriend walked in behind me to see who was in his house. I told him and her goodbye and left for my dad's house.

Forgive My Parents

As I grew through my forgiveness, I realized that as a 36-year-old southern gal, I respected my parents as adults because I had to, but I didn't respect them as parents. I said yes ma'am and no sir and called them Momma and Daddy, but I didn't respect their roles as my guardians.

Throughout my life as a child and an adult, I didn't have a relationship with my "real daddy," so I didn't know him very well. I wasn't sure why we didn't connect or why he wasn't around. Was it him? Was it my mom? Was it me? What I did know was that when I needed him the most he was never around.

It wasn't until I was around twelve years old that I figured out what a "real daddy" was. My sixth grade's sex education class taught me that a real daddy is the biological father. For me, he was the man that came into my life with broken promises and tried to buy my love with things like cassette players, radios, and golden arches kiddie meals. However, as I got older and closer with his brothers and sisters, I realized that he doesn't show love the way most people do with hugs, kisses, time and kind words. It was after many neglected moments and verbal abuse from him that I realized they were right. To me, the "real daddy" was just another adult I had to respect because he was an adult.

Eventually, my "real daddy" married a sweet woman with two kids. I saw how she and the kids changed him for the better. He became a father to her kids; however, our relationship didn't improve. After numerous attempts to make our relationship better, I got tired of trying. I reached the point where I was tired of begging a man, this man, to love me. So, I removed him from my life for a couple of years.

However, to get through my healing process, I wanted to mend our past because I felt I had one good shot left at having a relationship with him. That relationship had to begin with him answering why he neglected his role as my guardian.

I arrived at the house and walked in. I spoke to my stepmom and the kids. Then, I asked him to come outside to speak. We walked outside to the driveway.

"What are you doing here? I didn't know you were coming home." He stated.

I said, "Yeah, I wanted to talk to you about my childhood sexual abuse. When I first told you, I was twenty. You told me to 'get over it' and walked away with the coldest shoulder. Then, you asked my aunt if what I said was true. Even though she confirmed what happened, what you did only confirmed that you didn't believe me."

At that point, emotions started flooding my body and tears began to swell in my eyes.

Then I explained, "As a child, I was abused multiple times by multiple people. All I wanted was for someone to protect me, but you weren't there. Time after time, you lied to me about coming to get me. I would sit on the steps of the projects waiting for you to come, just for you to take me for a drive-thru meal and bring me right back home. Most of the time you didn't show up at all. Those lies hurt me. Those were the times I needed you. Why were you *not* there?"

He stood back looking at me. His eyes began to fill with tears as he stated, "I was young and dumb and made lots of mistakes. I didn't know. My mom tried to get you, but your mom wouldn't give you up. If I had known what you were going through, I would have fought harder. I'm so sorry."

As he continued to talk, I noticed a softer side of him I'd never seen before. My dad was a manly man—a coach with no sons only two daughters. He rarely showed loving and caring emotions towards me; however, here he was in front of me a softer and kinder man.

When he finished talking, he reached out to hug me. I went to him as a child, his child. As we stood there in his driveway embracing each other under the beautiful, bright, rays of the sun, he said, "I love you." I melted in his arms and cried like a little girl being held for the first time by her father.

We continued to stand in the driveway while talking, then he asked, "Have you spoken to your mom about this?"

I replied, "Yes."

He asked, "Did she tell you about what happened to her?"

I said, "Yes."

He said, "She didn't tell you everything. I know she didn't."

I looked at him confused. How did he know I needed to speak with her? It was another sign.

That was a mentally and emotionally exhausting day. I knew I needed to calm my nerves, ground my emotions and recharge for the carefrontation with my mother. So, before beginning again on Saturday, I took the Fourth of July, a Friday, to relax with one of my favorite positive sources of energy — my favorite cousin, Sheryl.

Sheryl's energy is loving, compassionate, caring and brutely honest. As an adult, I recharged with her whenever I could. After a day like that, I needed a recharge from her.

I knew the carefrontation with my mom was going to be the hardest. You see, I respected my mom as a provider. My mom was a sixth-grade dropout who was sexually, verbally and physically abused throughout her life before I was born. Afterwards, she became a hard-working woman with four kids who did what she could for us to have a roof over our heads. She was an awesome provider.

However, alcohol was her vice of choice to numb the pain of her past. Those vices resulted in her blindness to the signs of my abuse. So, I had anger towards her absence as my guardian. To heal, I wrote my letter of anger towards her and did my mantra to forgive her in my bathroom mirror. However, I also wanted a relationship with my mom. I mean…she's my mom.

That Saturday, July 5, I mentally prepared myself to have the conversation with my mom, but I just couldn't do it. My upbringing of not talking back to my mom still put fear in my heart. So, I figured I would wait until Sunday after I got my strength from church. After the days I'd had, I needed spiritual strength to face that carefrontation.

Then, at about 1:00 a.m. Sunday morning, my mom made her weekly liquid courage call to my voicemail where she vents about any and everything. However, instead of letting her call go to voicemail like I normally do, I answered the phone, "Hey, Momma."

She said, "I just want you to listen."

She went on to tell me her story—our family's story—a horrific story about a generational curse of childhood sexual abuse that went back over sixty years. As she spoke, I realized that it was the story of her, Rob, and Uncle's sexual abuse.

As she continued, tears streamed down my face and my heart raced to hear the pain of her being set on fire as a child for fighting against being sexually abused. She spoke about running away from home, the guilt she had from leaving her siblings behind, and staying in physically abusive relationships because she had nowhere else to go and how she copes with life. I couldn't believe it. My heart ached for her.

She talked about how she had me because she wanted someone to love her. Her love for me wouldn't allow anyone else to take me from her. So, she kept me with her.

Then, she got quiet.

I softly asked her, "What did you do when I told you about Uncle? Yeah, you kicked him out, but he still found me. What happened?"

As she explained her situation more, I mentally connected with the lie that I told myself. The lie was that my mom had the mental and emotional capabilities to protect me, but she just neglected me. The truth was that she didn't have the capabilities. She was a black woman growing up in the hood in the 60s, 70s and 80s who didn't know about mental health nor where to turn for mental health assistance to fight a generational curse.

Now I know why she drinks and why we never connected. I realized my mom needed a healing journey just like me.

As she talked, I just sat there and listened. Then, I responded, "Momma, what you went through wasn't your fault. You survived it, but now it's time for you to heal. Healing means getting the resources you need to forgive yourself and the feeling of abandonment of your siblings."

We talked for a little while longer before I said, "Momma, I love you for you. I understand you better now. Get some sleep and I will see you tomorrow before I leave."

After I hung up with my mom, I cried for her. However, her story enlightened me by answering the questions:

- Why wasn't she there? Work and alcohol were my mom's coping mechanisms for avoiding her emotions, the pain and the memories.

- Why didn't she protect me? Her emotional and mental barriers prevented her from moving past her hurt. In the '60s, '70s and '80s, brown girls lived in a time when there was limited information and resources available for mental health in the community.

That information changed my story that my mom didn't care about me. Yet, on my journey, I found quite the opposite. I uncovered a generational curse that was faced by avoidance, which didn't protect the next generations. I was no longer a brown girl who suffered childhood sexual abuse. I was a brown girl living under a generational curse where others were hurt and from which they didn't heal.

A generational curse is a very different struggle for brown girls. Dark memories and family secrets of generational curses are hard to overcome when a family wants to bury the narrative, the lies, the shame and the hurt. Well, as a stranger said to me, "A generational curse ran in my family until it ran into me." I stopped this curse in my family and hope to stop it with others. Trust me, breaking generational curses is *not* for the weak, but it can be done.

After speaking with my mom, I woke up on that Sunday morning feeling emotionally drained and needing a spiritual reconnection. I needed more than my traditional gospel playlist. I needed something stronger. I needed something Earth-shaking to get my energy back. I needed my pastor and close friends. I needed my church family. So, I went to my home church.

This was my first time stepping into my home church since before my pastor, Reverend Perry Posey, was killed in February 2002. You see, as a teenager, I joined the church to find answers and feel connected to a family. During that time, Reverend Posey became a supportive, caring and patient father figure. So, when he was murdered, I couldn't bring myself to return to church. Until that day.

When I arrived, I found that most of the church family was on a retreat; so, I sat with my church mother, Ma Debra. Church opened with the normal procedure of acknowledging visitors. I stood up to ask the church for prayer as I traveled my journey to heal from childhood sexual abuse.

It just so happened, that day the church had a female guest pastor. She stood up to do her sermon, not knowing me, my background or my history with the church. She told the story of how she struggled for days to develop a sermon and then on the night before, God sent her a message to give to me. In summary, His message was, "You are stronger than you think, and you will change the world with your testimony." I felt a chill come over me and my emotions became so overwhelming that I began to cry.

During altar call, I walked up and dropped to my knees to lay everything at the altar. Ma Debra came up to hold me as a mother does. She held me tight and told me to let it all go. I sat up on my knees and released my remaining emotions. I prayed for healing for my family and for myself. I asked God to continue to order my steps and guide me in His ways.

When I left church, I felt like a new, stronger woman. I felt free. The day I let it all go was July 6, 2014.

That Sunday was the most beautiful day. My dad called me just to talk and offered me a ride to the airport, which I gladly accepted. My mom called to tell me she was proud of me and my progress in my healing journey. That day the sun shined just a little bit brighter.

In conclusion, my experience and growth during this phase of my healing journey was life-altering. I forgave myself, my abusers and my parents, and I reconciled my relationships. I found my truth and ways to heal others. After my emotionally draining journey, I gained a new-found respect for my past and my strength, and I began to see life through a different lens.

The most valuable lesson you can learn in the Forgive Phase is to take the time and patience to go through it and grow through your emotions to find your courage, strength, and happiness.

LETTERS TO MY BROWN GIRLS

To My 10-Year-Old Self

Dear pretty brown girl,

It's me. Your 42-year-old self. I know 32 years from now seems far away and you don't think you will live to see 21, but you will.

Right now, you are hurting. But I'm here to tell you the pain will stop and you will never be hurt like that again.

Understand that *you* didn't do anything wrong. You went through what doctors call trauma. Trauma is a very bad injury to your mind, body or soul. The things that Uncle and Uncle #2 did to you caused trauma to you. *They* caused the trauma, so they are the ones with the issues, not you.

As you get older, you will face images from the trauma that will make you angry. I want you to know that having those images and that anger is normal. You are a human with emotions who experienced a trauma, so you should feel angry.

Right now, you are scared and have every right to feel that way. Even though you feel small, like Dr. Seuss said, "A person is still a person no matter how small." He was right. You are a person who is valuable to this world.

And guess what? Just like She-Ra, you have the power to heal the invisible pain. The journey we face to heal from this trauma is not easy, but *trust* me, you are stronger than you think.

You will use education and nature to heal. Education is like She-Ra's sword, a tool used to defend against evil thoughts and negativity in the world. Like She-Ra's shield, nature gives you a safe space to calm down, to love yourself and to heal. When everything else fails on your journey, education and nature always work to make you feel safe.

Here are pictures showing your bravery. Each picture has books at your feet or in your purse while enjoying nature. Look at you with weapons to take on the world.

You are a caring, respectful and loving person. You will show this through the ways you care for other children. Then, when you get older, you will show this kindness to those who hurt you. Even though you think they don't deserve your kindness, decide to show them kindness and accept them for who they are…human. Flawed humans. Your decision to show kindness is a huge step to healing and feeling better.

These steps are all a part of the healing process. These steps show your bravery to take on the world. You get braver every day that you face the world. All I ask is that you continue to be brave and have patience with yourself. Things will get better. Stay brave my 10-year-old She-Ra. Use your weapons wisely.

You got this. Take one step at a time.

Love,

Me

Letters to My Brown Girls

Little Brown Girls (brown girls under the age of 16)
To you, my little brown girl,

Good morning, my name is Cynthia. I hope your day is going ok. Mine is going ok, but I'm worried about you. Did you get my last letter that I wrote for brown girls like you? The one where I talked about private parts and sexual abuse.

Hopefully, you were brave enough to tell someone if you were sexually abused. After being sexually abused, you may feel scared, angry, and maybe nervous. I want you to know that it is normal to feel this way. Don't believe anyone when they tell you that you are not normal. What happened to you is not normal, but you are. Now, let's work on making you feel better.

The body is easy to heal once you stop the *source* of the pain from hurting you. So, the longer it takes for you to tell someone that you are being sexually abused, the longer the pain will last. To stop the pain, you have to say something as soon as possible. Do you understand? The only way to feel better is to tell someone until that person stops sexually abusing you. Now that I'm older, I wish I had told someone like a teacher or a guidance counselor, but as a kid, I didn't know better. As an adult, I know better. I know I could have stopped the sexual abuse if I would have told someone else.

If you feel you cannot trust anyone in your family, tell your teacher, a friend's parent, a guidance counselor or sometimes even a stranger, like a doctor, a police officer or a preacher. If you can't find any of them, I put phone numbers and internet addresses on www.hidntrezher.org to help you find someone. You can call the numbers, and someone will help to make the sexual abuse stop and find help to recover from the abuse.

My wish for you is to heal from being sexually abused. I know you are stronger than I was. Every day you show courage by placing your feet on the floor and getting out of bed to take on your day. Do *you* see the courage? Everyone couldn't get out of bed to face the unknowns of the day with your trauma, but you do. This means *each* day you face the world with *courage*. Even as a small person, you are brave. But again, it's like Dr. Seuss said, "A person is still a person no matter how small." He was right. You are a person who is valuable to this world.

I want today to be your last day of being sexually abused, but only you can stop the pain. I ask that you speak up. Speak up and let this be your first day living a courageous life away from sexual abuse.

XOXOXOXO

Another little brown girl,

Cynthia

Brown Girls (25 and over)

My Sister Queen,

Look at you! You are still here on this path less traveled; it is a healing journey from childhood sexual abuse. Some who went through what you went through did *not* survive. Take pride in knowing you could have given up long ago, but you didn't. You survived.

Now, you are moving from survival to becoming victorious over childhood sexual abuse and that requires forgiveness. Yes, you may feel that your attacker is unworthy of forgiveness. That feeling is expected. However, it is a feeling of anger.

Over the years, you lived with this anger. Anger allowed you to feel pain while not allowing the hurt to cut you too deeply. Anger protected you by absorbing the energy of others only for it to show up later in ways that weren't good for you. You can never repay anger for what it did for you when you needed it. Anger was your partner, but it's time for you to move past anger and its friends — fear, hurt, insecure and anxiety. Anger no longer serves a purpose in your life and must be released. Forgiving is the only way to release this anger for good.

You may feel like you can't find it in yourself to forgive what has been done to you, but you are stronger than you think. Forgiveness may even seem like a big step to you, and you are right. Forgiveness *is* a big step. Don't let anyone tell you any different. But guess what? You survived to live and grow, not to sulk in anger, hurt and insecurity.

One of my favorite quotes is, "Everybody wants to go to Heaven, but no one wants to die." It's my favorite quote because it signifies how you can't accomplish your greatest goals without putting in the hard work. The hard work of healing includes forgiving. So, let's do it.

Let's start with the fact that you provide value to this world. Regardless of your money, size, type of hair, skin color or the sexual abuse you experienced, you bring a unique and irreplaceable value to this world. The world deserves the best of you, and you can't give your best if you are pushing negativity off on everyone around you.

You do deserve peace. You deserve peace of mind so that you can make space to learn about yourself and the wonders this world has to offer. You deserve peace of mind so that you can become a version of yourself that is patient with your decisions, your actions and your outcomes. You deserve peace.

Once you make the decision to forgive, your next step is to forgive through the Forgive Exercise in this book. You release the built-up anger and resentment you have towards the person who sexually abused you. Yes, I know this sounds impossible, but you can do it.

Let's make the decision to let this anger go from your mind and spirit, and for it to never return to your body, heart and mind. It's your decision to make and you don't have to tell anyone about it. If you didn't go through the exercise yet, when you are ready, just do it.

Once you release the anger, don't go back to it. Don't lean on it. Don't use it as a crutch. That is not who you are anymore.

Forgive because you are a valuable, strong, brave and resilient brown queen. You can do this because you came this far and are ready to take it to the next level. Know that I love you and I believe in you. I will see you on the other side of forgiveness.

Sincerely,

Your sister in healing

CHAPTER 3

Transition Phase

Dear Sister Queen,
As you get older, you assess your life. You may ask yourself, *Why can't I be happy? Why can't I relax? Why do I keep hurting myself?* Or you may just think, *Something in my life just isn't right.* Negative feelings and events just keep happening and you can't quite put your finger on why. Yet, you stay in the cycle of what you know and don't investigate the why.

From the moment you were abused as a child, your response to life that included a constant state of anxiety and fear in the backdrop because you were scared that you were going to be abused again. From then on, your response to the anxiety and fear was to either fight, run or just freeze up. When trauma from your childhood sexual abuse goes unaddressed, you grow up feeling that anxiety and fear is normal and you view responses of fighting, running, or freezing as normal activities.

As you got older, that underlying feeling and response made it hard for you to sleep, relax or find peace in the calm. You did things like fight and argue with people over little or irrelevant things to keep drama in your life, you distanced yourself from healthy relationships, or you froze a part of your life that gave you comfort in the anxiety, anger or fear. These things became acceptable behavior. Normal behavior. This is your answer to the "whys."

Like any other animal in a toxic environment, your responses became habits to help you live in your habitat. It's what you knew. Whether healthy or unhealthy, your habits were built to help you survive everyday life for the environment you were in.

In toxic habitats, unhealthy responses to stress, anxiety, or pain from childhood sexual abuse include consuming drugs, drinking alcohol, self-sabotage, procrastination, fighting constantly, risky sexual behavior or abusive relationships. The problem is that once the fighting is over and the high, the buzz or the sex partner is gone, the stress, anxiety and pain are still there. These habits were or may still be your survival tactics. However, now that you are out of the sexual abuse, those unhealthy habits are no longer needed. So, it's time to replace those unhealthy habits with healthy habits.

In Phase 3: the Transition Phase, you transition from a survivor to a victor by altering your habits to reflect the positive and healthy life you want based on a freed mindset—not one trapped under the weight of childhood sexual abuse. To start, you evaluate your habits. A habit consists of three parts: a trigger (anything that starts a response), a response (your actions), and the output (what you receive). When you break a habit down into its parts, you can target each part to understand how to change your habits. In this phase, you identify your unhealthy responses caused by the trauma of childhood sexual abuse, create boundaries and standards to keep your mind on a healthy path and replace your unhealthy and negative responses with healthier and positive responses. The goal is to become self-sufficient in controlling your thoughts, emotions and actions.

Phase 3: Transition Phase is accomplished by keeping the Transition Rule in the front of your thinking. The Transition Rule is: *You cannot 100% control what happens to you; however, you can 100% control how you respond.* Here you will learn how to control yourself, how to give yourself happiness, and how to deal with the ups and downs of life using your own tools. The key to transitioning from a survivor to a victor is focusing on *your* responses for your new environment.

For example, stress can be triggered by many sources. Stress triggers many people to perform unhealthy habits of drinking alcohol (response) to numb the pain of hurt (output) or to feel relaxed (output). However, the effects of drinking alcohol provide temporary reliefs of stress and are unhealthy for the body. The output of less stress can be achieved by other responses such as working out, taking a walk, or solving the root cause of the stress.

Like you, I was on the same path. It took me a while to see my unhealthy responses to my triggers. My teenage and young adult years shaped my habits. My memories provide examples of unhealthy responses and their triggers.

MEMORIES

Memory 10: My First Love

The summer of '91 was memorable. It was the summer of my rights of passage from a little girl to a teenager. I graduated from elementary school, saw porn for the first time, and turned thirteen, and my babysitting services were booming. It was also the summer that I found my first love. It was a summer to remember.

South Carolina summers brought heat and the southern coma. After playing in the southern sun, a nap under the box fan in my window was the answer. The comatose nap hit me as soon as I laid in the bed.

While sleeping, I was awakened by someone slowly pulling on my underwear. Immediately, fear paralyzed my body as my panties were tugged downwards. As I tightened my legs closed, hands tried to force them open, but I was able to keep them closed. I opened my eyes to see my cousin, Ted. I screamed and kicked hysterically until he ran out the door.

Left alone in my room with my fears and anxiety, tears began to stream down my face. I was tired of the sexual abuse, loneliness and just life. My family constantly made jokes about my slanted eyes and called me white girl for the way I spoke. Boys terrorized me all the time; they pushed on me and called me Swamp Thing and Nerd. Every man I knew hurt me. I was tired and life just wasn't worth living anymore.

I thought that if I died, no one would even miss me. I had no future, so why continue living? So, I dried my tears and went into the bathroom. There it was under the sink — a poison to take the pain away. I kneeled, picked up the bottle and slowly put it to my lips. As I lifted the bottle to drink, a voice inside of me said, *Stop. If you die, who will watch over BabyDoll? You can't leave her or the other kids. Even if no one else loves you, they do.* I stood up, looked in the mirror, wiped the tears from my face and left for Maggie's house.

The short walk to Maggie's was one of hurt, embarrassment and depression. After walking into the apartment, my body plopped onto the couch by the door and rolled up into the fetal position. Maggie looked at me with concern and asked, "Are you ok? I got cookies." I didn't feel like having any cookies. "You can eat some with Baby-Doll," she insisted. I looked down and there she was, Baby-Doll, playing on the floor.

I got up and laid down with her. As Maggie prepared cookies, BabyDoll and I played patty cake with my face. She giggled every time she popped spit out of my mouth. That was what I needed to make me feel better. At least I knew that Maggie and BabyDoll loved me. From then on, Maggie's safe house became my home and BabyDoll was my heart.

Memory 11: A Guardian Angel

Summer was over, which meant the start of school. I was starting middle school. It was three blocks away from the projects, which meant I didn't have to ride a school bus with the bullies anymore. It was an opportunity to be a new me. After years of being picked on for being me, I did not want to be me anymore, so I decided to not be a nerd anymore. I invented a new me. It was a new beginning.

Throughout seventh grade, I didn't do any work and made bad grades. No one knew or cared. I was late for class, I hung out in the halls, and I did what I wanted to do. Then one day *she* caught me.

I was playing in the hallway when a God-like voice said, "Young lady, what are you doing and where are you supposed to be? Come here now!"

It was the principal, Dr. McFadden.

She said, "What's your name young lady?"

"Cynthia," I replied.

"I'm seeing you in my halls too much. If I see you again, you *will* come to my office and explain why you are not in class and in *my* halls," she said.

"Yes ma'am," I replied and thought, *She's not going to catch me again. I'll switch halls. She won't remember what she said.*

I walked away foolishly ignoring her statement.

About a week later, I was playing in the halls again.

The God-like voice came again saying, "Cynthia, what did I say? In my office, now!"

Dang it, she caught me. The face-down march to her office was embarrassing.

I was sitting in the front office when she came in and said, "Get in my office now."

I walked into her office as she pulled out a stack of papers.

She looked at me and said, "Who do you think you're fooling? I see what you are doing. I pulled your elementary test scores and grades plus your current work. I talked to your teachers. You are smart, but you aren't applying yourself. What's going on with you? Why did you come here and start making bad grades? Why are you not trying?"

I stated, "I just don't want to."

Then, she went on a rant for however long.

When I started listening again, she finished by saying, "I'm not going to let you quit, even if I have to stay on you every single day. I will call you out in the hallway. I will push you to try harder. Now, go around to the guidance office and introduce yourself to the counselors. Let them know I sent you."

From then on, that woman *never* let up. She stayed on me. Between her and the guidance counselors, Mrs. Cleveland and Mrs. Littejohn, they introduced me to college and told me that being smart would provide me with a way out of no way. They even said, "You could go to college." I didn't know I could go to college. I mean, I heard about it on "The Cosby Show" and saw it on "A Different World," but I never thought I could go. My parents weren't doctors or lawyers. But they said I could go, so I believed them. From that point on, I learned my teachers and principals could be friends too. Even if they were mean, they cared just as much.

Memory 12: Looking for Love

The journey from seventh to nineth grade was a blur of mistakes; however, my kids kept me sane. They distracted me from the anxiety, fear and embarrassment of the sexual abuse that showed up during the nights and in interactions with people. It's like my emotions and fears got worse in middle school.

Babysitting worked well until my ninth-grade year when my mom moved us from Tank Branch into a house on the east side of the railroad tracks. We moved into a new house right before I started tenth grade. New house and new school meant new friends and a new beginning. I hung out with my new friends and went to football games and parties, but at night, fear, anxiety and loneliness were still there.

As time went on, my babysitting jobs started to dwindle which meant no more kids to love. My kids were big and didn't need me anymore.

To keep my mind calm and occupied, I stayed at school for sporting events, helped with after-school programs and went to friends' homes to hang out. But then, in the summer of '96, my last set of kids aged out of my care, so my services were no longer needed. It was over. What was I going to do?

I wanted someone to love me unconditionally, someone to call my own and someone I could trust. So I thought, *I'll have a baby*. I knew I could be the best mommy ever. I would help my child with homework, cook dinner and take care of them when they were sick. Most importantly, I would never work second or third shift jobs because I needed to be there to protect them. So, my boyfriend and I made the decision to have a baby.

So now, here I was a senior in high school, pregnant. However, my boyfriend later made other plans that didn't include a baby. I was upset, but I knew I had to take responsibility for my decision and my life. I knew what I wanted. At least, I thought I knew.

Being a teenage mom in high school with dual-credit classes of calculus (advanced placement) and college English was hard as hell. Stress hit me hard. I was surrounded by negativity from home and school—my grandma telling me I will never make it in this world, my real dad calling me stupid and foolish, and my calculus teacher telling me I wasn't smart enough to make it in college. Stress caused a two-month premature delivery of a beautiful little boy.

He was the most wonderful thing I ever saw. He became my world. So, I couldn't give up. I had to stay focused enough to graduate and get into college. The negativity I received fueled me to work harder and find ways to provide for my son.

Memory 13: Teenage Mom

The birth of my son strengthened my relationships with my positive sources of energy—my like-minded friends. My friends and their parents motivated me in ways my family couldn't. Reverend Posey provided fatherly guidance as I navigated my fear and anxiety of being a teenage mom and my future. I would visit the local restaurant, Little Moo, or his car wash to get advice. He hugged me and told me how to navigate my thoughts.

Ma Elnora, Ma Debra, and Momma Pon gave me motherly advice when I needed it and when I didn't want to hear it. On really bad days, I walked the half mile to Ma Elnora's house just to see her face and hear her voice, and sometimes just to be in her presence. There were many days I cried to her about my nightmares, fears, anxieties and thoughts. However, she poured her love, patience and understanding back into me. Her hugs were food to my soul. Those sources of energy made being a teenage mom bearable. I returned to those sources of energy every chance I could.

When I graduated in 1997, I knew it was time for me to grow up. My "real daddy" got me a summer job at the local trucking company. So, as my friends prepared for Senior Week at Myrtle Beach, I prepared to start a summer job. Graduation was on a Wednesday. The job started Monday.

Over the summer, I saved my money to move into my own place. When the summer ended, money was still short, so I got a student loan to get a car to drive to school and daycare.

Being a teenage mom was hard, but being a single, first-time mom and freshman college student was harder. Jesus! Trying to find a babysitter while I went to school and work-study was a daily chore. With hardly any help from my family, I had to lean on my friends. They were so supportive, but they were just like me—teenagers. There were many times I wanted to just quit. I made barely enough money for a rental assistance apartment and made too much money for a livable amount of welfare. Dealing with the welfare system was frustrating, but it was necessary to get childcare vouchers so I could go to school.

Memory 14: My First Time

As my freshman year of college ended, the trucking company offered me another summer job. Things started to get better for me. So, considering that I had a job, a car and an apartment with actual furniture, I felt it was time for me to deal with my childhood sexual abuse.

To start my healing journey, I went to the county mental health clinic to see what I could do to address my issues from childhood sexual abuse. That was my first time seeking help, and I didn't know what to expect. The doctor was a white lady in her late twenties or early thirties who sat there and listened. Her feedback was never relatable. It was like she just didn't get me. Then, after two sessions, she prescribed medication for me. I'd never heard of the drug and I didn't like taking pills. However, the doctor said it would help me. So, I took the medicine.

Man, what did I do that for? I took it at 7:00 a.m. before I went to work, thinking I was going to be okay. By mid-morning, my heart was racing. My head was spinning. My hands were jittery. Anxiety consumed my entire body. I knew I had to get away because I was working around heavy machinery.

The "real daddy" worked at the trucking company, so I looked for him to see if he could help me. When I found him, I explained to him about the sexual abuse, my healing journey, the doctor and the medicine. He looked at me and said, "Get over it. It's in the past!"

His response shocked me. I couldn't believe he'd said that to me. He was so cold. As tears built up in my eyes, I ran into the bathroom and sat on the floor crying and shaking. I thought I was going to lose my fucking mind. I didn't know what to do.

As I sat there crying, a woman came in and saw me. She turned around and left to find my aunt who also worked at the trucking company. My aunt came in and asked what was wrong. I told her about being sexually abused and the medicine. Slowly, she helped me up and walked me to the Human Resources (HR) office to inform them of my state. HR told me to go home and rest.

I didn't feel safe enough to drive, so I called my boyfriend to come take me home. He took me to his place to rest so he could watch over me. After the medicine wore off, I woke up. I sat in the bed and told him what happened. His eyes showed compassion and understanding. He patiently listened to me while comforting me. That's what I needed.

I learned a couple of lessons that day: Not all doctors are created equal, don't deal with doctors who don't investigate the root cause of mental issues before putting you on medication, a certain medication was not for me, and

I didn't want to deal with my sexual abuse issues again anytime soon.

In closing, these memories reflected my need for mental health resources; however, I was not aware that mental health was supposed to be an acceptable thing during those times. Diving deep into these memories made me want to know more about healthy responses for addressing and healing from childhood sexual abuse and heal past the mistakes I made as a teenager.

DID YOU KNOW

Childhood sexual abuse *is* a mental health issue. It impacts how a child thinks, acts and feels as they grow up (CDC, 2021). When a child is sexually abused, their brain immediately releases cortisol, a stress hormone that serves as the brain's alarm system to the rest of the body. This alarm indicates that the body is experiencing a threat. This causes the heart to start to race and move blood from the other main organs to all the muscles that the body needs to fight, flight or freeze.

Now, imagine what happens to a child's developing body that is on constant high alert from fear of being sexually abused again. This keeps the nervous system on high alert and results in the anxiety, fear, and anger we feel as childhood sexual abuse survivors.

This type of trauma mandates that you get mental help just to pull you through the anxiety of life and the anxiety triggered by thoughts of the abuse. Think about it. Without mental help, the memories and anxiety can play out in your thoughts repeatedly over a day, a month, and even decades as you saw in Chapter 1 and Chapter 2.

The problem is that as a brown girl growing up in the south, I was exposed to a cultural mistrust of mental help. In the black community you are told, "Black people don't go sit on somebody's couch. They go see the pastor or talk to their barber or stylist." This is how my culture describes seeking mental help from a "trained specialist." Another example is when someone says, "Black people don't have mental issues." That's the same someone who says, "You know she touched in the head." This is our way of saying someone needs mental help. These beliefs make a person like me feel ashamed for seeking mental help.

What happens when you don't address the fear, anxiety or anger from childhood sexual abuse? According to the CDC (2021), results of childhood sexual abuse include unwanted pregnancies, heart disease, obesity, depression, substance abuse, risky sexual behavior, chronic anxiety and suicide attempts. It's these types of responses to sexual abuse that supports the CDC's statement that the total economic burden of child sexual abuse to the United States economy was estimated above $9.3 billion in 2015.

Negative responses to childhood sexual abuse are the reasons why we need mental health awareness and support in our communities. To be clear, I wholeheartedly support mental health because it is only a fourth of holistic healing. Mental, physical, emotional and spiritual healing are my components of holistic healing. Each one is needed.

As previously stated, I didn't always believe in mental health. My belief system changed when I changed my environment. The toxic negativity or what some call the "crabs in a barrel" mentality wouldn't allow me to see the benefits of "sitting on someone's couch." Believe me, sometimes you need to seek mental health assistance.

As a sexual abuse survivor, some days you experience more hurtful thoughts than other days. You and I both know people fight the good fight daily to stay positive; however, the fight isn't always easy. As negative thoughts enter your mind and emotions consume you, you need resources that can guide your responses to the positive side.

In the Phase 3: Transition Exercise, you focus on your mental health from the perspective of habits. Habits are responses we create based on what happens in our environment. Each habit has a trigger which causes you to respond with certain actions to achieve a certain output. Let's get started with changing the unhealthy responses to healthy and positive responses.

PHASE 3: TRANSITION EXERCISE

In this Phase 3, the Transition Phase, you transition from a survivor to a victor by focusing on your habits. A habit consists of three parts: a trigger (anything that starts a response), a response (your actions), and the output (what you receive). When you break a habit down into its parts, you can target each part to understand how to change your habits. The goal is to become self-sufficient in controlling your thoughts, emotions and actions.

The Transition Phase starts with modifying or creating your bedtime routine and morning ritual. A bedtime routine is a set of actions you do before bed to clear your mind in preparation for sleep and preparation for the next day. A morning ritual is a set of actions you do to prepare you for the day. These actions give you time and space to prepare for and respond to your day.

Part of your Transition Phase is setting up your journal to write during your bedtime routine and to recall during your morning ritual. For this phase, you will need a notebook to develop your Habit Table (Appendix F) and a pen. For the next two weeks, journal your activities daily for an hour as part of your bedtime routine and review it in the morning to ensure it is accurate.

When writing, break down each activity to identify your mental, emotional and physical responses to stress, anxiety, loneliness or any other emotion or action you may have. For example, "Today the rainy day made me feel depressed and lonely, so I decided to get a bottle of wine and drink while watching a movie." This phase will not work if you are not honest with yourself, so make sure to journal everything.

This part of the activity is the exploration of your response to events in daily life and why you respond the way you do. After journaling for two weeks, create a Habit Table with four columns to input each activity and each of the three elements of habit: trigger (what happened), response (what did you do?), and output (what did you receive?). Break down each activity into the Habit Table. Now, journal for another two weeks using the Habit Table.

Date	Trigger	Response	Outputs
11/10/16	Rainy day	Felt depressed and lonely. Drank a bottle of wine while watching TV.	Distracted from being lonely.

Next, set boundaries and standards to shape your thoughts and actions for how you live going forward. This is where you identify how *you* want to live your life. Boundaries are how far left and right you go in your decisions and actions. For example, you can set the boundaries to choose people who feed you (right boundary) over people who bleed you (left boundary). Standards are the lowest levels that you go. They are the non-negotiables in your life. For example, you don't get to choose the kind of people you have in your family (lowest standard), but you can choose the kind of people you have as your friends (highest standard for the quality of people). For me, my family members included drama queens, alcoholics, drug dealers, pedophiles, and thieves; however, I chose to be around positive family members like police officers, teachers, and pastors.

Next, review your table of triggers, responses and outputs for unhealthy triggers, responses and outputs. If you have triggers that you *can* control, then control them using your standards and boundaries. For example, the smell of beer triggered my childhood sexual abuse memories. Therefore, I had a standard to not date men who drank beer or smoked cigarettes. Those are my standards and are non-negotiable.

For those triggers that you *can't* control, evaluate your *response*. Then use your standards and boundaries to replace your negative responses with a healthier or a positive response. For example, one of my old triggers used to be sexual assault-type videos. The Army requires every soldier to attend sexual assault awareness training during boot camp. As I watched the video of sexual assault, my anxiety began to build (negative response). To escape the trigger, I removed the source of anxiety from my view by walking out of training (negative response). However, my employer still had a requirement to increase employee's awareness of sexual assault. This requirement was met by watching a sexual assault video (trigger) to receive proof that I was aware of sexual assault in the military and knew how to prevent it and report it (output).

So as a soldier or an employee, I had to find a healthy response (no anxiety) to this uncontrollable trigger. My response was to heal from my sexual abuse (healthy response) as I did in Phases 1 and 2. Now, sexual assault videos don't bother me, and I successfully complete each employer's sexual assault awareness training requirement.

For those triggers that you *can't* control that result in *unhealthy* outputs, you set boundaries and standards to change the unhealthy response and unhealthy responses. For example, childhood sexual abuse left me feeling unworthy to be loved. Whenever I had a fight with my "real daddy" (trigger), this unworthiness (output) triggered loneliness (output). My unhealthy response was to turn to the arms of Mr. Wrong. Even though he provided the output I needed not to feel lonely, my action wasn't a healthy, long-term response for feeling worthy and being sufficient for myself. When I was twenty-six, I temporarily removed that trigger from my life and reduced communications to just texting during the holidays. This removed that unhealthy response and gave me time and space to heal.

My healthier response was setting standards and boundaries for how I treated myself and loved myself and for how others treated me. As I grew through my triggers, responses and outputs, I outgrew negative people, severed one-way relationships and disconnected from negative and selfish family members. This freed space in my thoughts, emotions and heart to focus more on my health and mental well-being.

You will find that each trigger, response and output that you face is different; therefore, you need an arsenal of tools that work for you at any given moment for any habit element. For example, replace risky sexual behavior with walking, running, painting or some other craft that allows you to release negative energy you are experiencing. Have patience with yourself as you create a list of the replacements and try each of them until you find the one that works for you. You will know you found the right replacement when it cultivates your soul, guides your spirit when you feel lost, or inspires you to be better. This phase of the healing journey takes deep personal reflection, then courage, then personal reflection, then courage, then personal reflection, then courage. You get my point.

I will warn you that replacing elements of habit is a daily, if not hourly, practice and adjusting habits isn't something that you can do in a week or two. Remember that you are attempting to change emotions and habits that you have used for years. It takes at least twenty-one days of constant effort to make minor changes to habits and one to three years for major changes in your life. So, have patience and focus on progression not perfection.

Also, I'm not saying you won't ever feel tired or stressed again, but as negative energy and habits creep back into your thoughts, emotions, arms or bed, you need the right tool to react in a healthy way. Eventually, you will begin to take a deep breath to slow yourself down prior to making any decisions so that you can evaluate how to respond. Then, look to your toolkit of responses to respond with positive, healthy actions. Finally, you will get to a point where you are whole, healthy and happy on more days than you feel empty, stressed, depressed or lonely.

These actions initiate a chain reaction of positive behavior and energy in other parts of your life. For example, you may choose to meditate to calm your mind. Meditation is also good for learning how to control your emotions while also making you more aware of your body. As the chain reaction occurs, you may not see positive effects immediately, but you will feel the positive energy grow. When your positivity and healthy habits overtake the negative energy, thoughts and emotions, and you have patience with yourself, your transition from a survivor to a victor is complete.

EXPERIENCE AND GROWTH

To move beyond the hurt, I removed myself from the triggers of my trapped memories and emotions. I knew that to be a better me, I needed space to be able to make mistakes and analyze them without someone putting negative energy into my thoughts and growth. So, I left for D.C. in 2004.

The migration north to D.C. initiated a year of efforts to liberate myself from unhealthy habits and negative people. New habits included things like eating healthier or as my stepdad called it eating rabbit food. Another habit was unhealthy dating habits. I didn't date for a year because I recognized my daddy issues triggering me to go back to the wrong type of guys, so I had to break that habit slowly. That was a hard one to do.

The space and time away from triggers allowed me to heal on my own time. My unhealthy habits of procrastination and late bill paying changed to structure, planning, scheduling and effective execution of tasks in my personal life which trickled into my career. My new habits, healthy responses and new positive attitude grew because I was in an environment that I shaped, not one shaped by my past. My habits resulted in the completion of a Bachelor of Science after seven years and dropping out of college twice, the attainment of a Master of Science in Network Security, being open to love, and getting my doctorate of science in cybersecurity. All of this because of positive and healthy boundaries and standards that created healthy habits.

Habits are interesting things to study. They provide valuable insights into who you really are. As you go through your exercises, know that you may not get it right the first time or even the second time. Take the time to patiently wait on yourself as you transition into your new role as a victor. It will be worth the wait. Remember to focus on progression, not perfection, and that the only thing you can control 100 percent is you.

LETTERS TO MY BROWN GIRLS *(Under 25)*

Hey pretty brown girl,

Someone special gave you this letter because they feel you and I are connected by a similar life-altering experience. So, many days ago, I decided to write you this letter to guide you through this life-altering event that you may have experienced.

See, I was sexually abused as a child for years, and your special someone thinks you were sexually abused as well. Before you respond...pause for a second. If you haven't been sexually abused, then thank your special person for their concern. Everyone isn't as caring as the person who gave you this letter. Just say thank you and move on.

Now, if you were sexually abused, then thank the person for their compassion because everyone doesn't care enough to notice signs of childhood sexual abuse plus follow up to check on you. Make sure you thank them for watching over you.

See unlike most adults, I have *no* issues with speaking to you about what you went through because I've experienced and healed from childhood sexual abuse. That's the reason for this letter.

As I wrote this letter, I thought about how to best offer you help with what you may be going through. From the time I was sexually abused and even after it stopped, I felt broken, lost and empty. Sometimes, I was consumed by so much negative energy that I felt numb to the world and lived my life as if the next day didn't exist. The negative energy and thoughts led me to an attempt at suicide as a teenager, self-injury using risky sexual behavior and dropping out of college twice. I alienated myself because I didn't want to face the memories, emotions or forgiveness. So, because of all of that, I realized I'm the best person to write you because I still remember what it was like being a young brown girl who was sexually abused. I know what lies ahead for you if you don't take the time and space to heal.

I also know what the possibilities look like on the other side of healing from childhood sexual abuse. This letter came from a book, *Letters to My Brown Girls*. The book provides brown girls in adult bodies over the age of twenty-five guidance on their journey to heal from their abuse. However, I couldn't ignore you — the young brown girl who has yet to face what older women faced — the memories, sounds, and smells of your abuse can cause you to create unhealthy ways to deal with reminders. I promise you that it's not a matter of *if* the triggers will come, because they *will* come. It's a matter of how *you* will respond to them when they come.

This letter is here to help guide you through these triggers to find your source of happiness, lead a healthy life and prepare for a brighter future. So, I ask that you give me five minutes of your undivided attention. I promise this won't take long. When you're done, you can ask your special someone for more information or you can go back to your day. Five minutes is all I ask, and I will respect your time.

To start, I'm upset you experienced this horrible event. No child should ever have to go through sexual abuse. It can really mess a person up. The damages to your body will heal with time, but your mind and soul will take a lot longer to heal.

Due to your sexual abuse, triggers to the thoughts and emotions of your sexual abuse can pop up any day and any time—while you're sleeping, when you are speaking to someone, or when you are watching TV. These triggers can cause your mood to change quickly. If you don't know how to handle them, you may do something that you will regret later. The key to healing from childhood sexual abuse is how you respond to these triggers.

Up until I was twenty-six, my emotions, thoughts and actions were shaped by the anxiety, anger and fear of being sexually abused. These emotions make you feel like no one will ever want you and that no one cares. These things are not true.

Those emotions and thoughts are what adults call smoke and mirrors. Emotions of anxiety and fear are the smoke that clouds your thinking. You feel embarrassed about the abuse and think no one else will understand you. This is the smoke. The negative thoughts are mirrors that make you look at yourself and think you are the only one who has experienced childhood sexual abuse or that you are not worthy of love. Even though these smoke and mirrors are normal for what you've been through, they are not the truth.

If the smoke and mirrors go unchecked now, you will live life feeling damaged, unvaluable and lost. You will constantly look for something, anything, to make yourself feel better. This will make it difficult for you to see the truth about yourself and your value to the world. However, you can make the decision to blow through the smoke and break all the mirrors.

You are not alone in this world nor are you the only one who has experienced childhood sexual abuse. There are survivors just like you. During my healing journey, I met countless brown girls in adult bodies who were sexually abused. Like me, they also struggled to start, go through and make it out of the anger and pain from sexual abuse.

I ask that you take some time to read my story. As you read it, you will notice that even though my healing journey was long, I became a more loving, caring, self-respecting and self-sufficient woman because of it. Follow my healing journey and try my method of healing for yourself. If it doesn't work for you, there are plenty of resources in this book to help you heal in private at home or in public with group support. If you still cannot find a support group, visit www.hidntrezher.org to request the creation of a support group. I will see what I can do to help you form one or form one for you.

My wish for you is to heal. I know you can do it because you came from a long line of survivors. Your ancestors didn't lay down or give up, so you can't give up because of what life throws at you. You are here because they were strong enough to make it through oppression, civil war, diseases, racism, and sexism to bring you into this world.

As a victor, I want you to heal so that you can show the world who you are—a beautifully made brown princess who is ready to take on the world and give it the best you got. Know that I love you, I believe in you, and you are *not* alone in this journey. Hope to connect with you one day. Smile and enjoy your day.

Love,
Cynthia

Brown Girls (Over 25)

Good morning sister queen,

It is 5:38 a.m., and I'm in mid-swing of my morning ritual. It's funny how our minds solve problems during our sleep and we wake up with solutions. My morning ritual was and still is my best tool for being successful. It is what produced my healing journey, my dissertation, building global cyber programs, this book and now this letter.

You made it through the end of this chapter; however, if you are doing the exercises, I know you are just getting started with your Transition Phase. This phase takes time and patience for you to truly reflect on you. Please take your time especially with the current uncontrollable triggers playing out in the news. The emotions of the #BlackLivesMatter movement against the 800-year expansion of the British empire and the #MeToo Movement's efforts to fight against sexual abuse can be straining to our mental health.

Being a brown girl isn't easy and when you add childhood sexual abuse on top of just being brown, well, life can be downright unbearable at times, so you just want to cry. However, it is our history of adversity and strength that makes rhythm and blues (R&B), blues and gospel music just feel different than other types of music. It is this music and those feelings that lifts us over our struggles of just being brown. And these days, we *must* take a break from being strong and *just* focus on our mental health.

As a childhood sexual survivor, you created survival tactics to handle the mental and emotional triggers in your life, but now, you no longer need those unhealthy tactics. In the Transition Phase of healing, you read about healing past your triggers and survival tactics to become a victor over your childhood sexual abuse. I must warn you that this part is not going to be easy. It's hard to identify and break away from habits and tactics you formed to numb the pain, calm the anxiety and release your anger from being sexually abused. So, take your time and have patience with yourself.

As you grow through your experiences of this chapter, use the Habit Table (Appendix F) or build one using large Post-it notes or a whiteboard. Once you identify your unhealthy response, try multiple healthy responses until you find the one that works for you. If a standard or boundary doesn't work for you, then try another one. Don't give up. Remember: progression not perfection.

This book is an example of my triggers of memories and emotions, my struggles with responses and what worked for me to change my habits and transition. And let me tell you, the struggle was real. While breaking down my habits, I realized my triggers caused many emotions. My responses included paying bills late when I had money and time to pay them on time, starting arguments for no reason just to cause pain, and sabotaging myself by not showing up for meetings and procrastinating. During those trying times, I couldn't live my day without stress and anxiety, so I kept it going.

When I began to build my healthy responses, I collected many types of positive routines and tools because I never knew what tool I would need on any given day. For example, I replaced paying bills late with creating a budget with a schedule of all bills to pay them on time, separating bank accounts for different reasons, creating an emergency fund for unplanned bills, and setting up auto bill pay. All of these responses were to remove some stress and anxiety from my life.

To introduce positivity into my life, negative energy was replaced with sources of positive energy. I created an online video playlist called Morning Ritual that I watched or listened to while I prepared for the day. Check out my Morning Ritual video playlist at www.hidntrezher.org.

I will tell you that breaking down and replacing habits isn't something I figured out over a week or a month. Changing habits took me years (some took months) to do because I took the time to be honest with myself and acknowledge my truth. My fears and anger created excuses for being lazy and procrastinating, and self-sabotaging kept me and my attitude down. That all changed as I went through the Transition Phase.

For you to become a victor, you will go through the same journey. Your patience is key for growth through this journey, and growth will come in many forms. This is where you transition your life to the one you want to live and be present in. One day, this transition will be something to step back and look at and realize how far you've grown.

Stay strong in your decision to continue the transition to a victor. Growth comes in the journey. Remember as you transition, focus on progression, not perfection.

Love,
Cynthia

CHAPTER 4

Rebirth Phase

Dear Sister Queen,
In Phase 3: Transition Phase, you began your transition from unhealthy to healthy habits using boundaries and standards to build a positive and healthy life. Once you get to a point where your positivity and healthy habits occur *more* than your negative habits and negative energy, you have proven to yourself that your transition is complete. Now, it's time for you to take your habits, your standards, and your boundaries and build a new environment for the new you—the victorious, resilient you.

In the Phase 4: Rebirth Phase, you are reborn into the environment shaped by your new boundaries, standards, and views. This is done through spiritual transformation, living in your truth and living a purposeful life. The goal is to build the life you want based on the new you—your boundaries, your non-negotiables, your views and your purpose.

With that being said, I struggled with my rebirth. Major professional challenges almost put me back in my old habits. I had to kill the old me to move forward in my transition and be reborn, but the rebirth was worth it. Witness the rebirth…

MEMORIES

Memory 15: Really, God

After my forgiveness journey to South Carolina, I returned home with a new sense of confidence and pride. I was more aware of myself and that was the best feeling ever. I had faced my deepest, darkest memories, emotions and fears.

My return to work had me feeling like I was sitting on top of the world, but then the uncontrollable triggers started. The replacement of my latino female boss with a new, white male boss gave off vibes that felt all too familiar as a brown girl from the South. From the day he started, he would only talk to me in meetings. As we passed each other in the hall, I spoke to him yet he wouldn't look me in the face or return a common courtesy of hello. When he did speak to me, it was in meetings only. It was ridiculous, but I was on probation and wanted to keep my job. So, I stayed focused on my goal.

However, when he partnered with two co-workers from another department, co-worker 1 (CW1) and co-worker 2 (CW2), their microaggressions made work damn near intolerable. I knew why, but I wasn't going to let them see this brown girl sweat. I had been through too much over the summer to give in to them.

One day though, I almost called it quits. In a moment of frustration, I went to a longtime friend, Doug, who was also a co-worker. As I vented my frustration to Doug, he looked at me and said, "Cynthia, you my girl and all but you have to stay put."

I looked at him thinking, *What the hell?*

I replied, "Doug, I could make twice as much money with the same headache or less headache."

He said, "Yeah, but that's not what's for you right now. You must take one for the team and stay put. See, one day, you will be a symbol of hope and pride for those that look like you. Don't leave. You can handle them. Just take one for the team."

I had worked with Doug for five years. He's never misguided me. So, I took that as a sign to stay put and let their microaggressions polish me. I would learn how to deal with them to teach those coming after me. So, I took a couple for the team.

Then one day, my boss called me on the phone and said, "I need you to attend this cybersecurity meeting at the Pentagon because CW1 is out of the office. The meeting is in two hours."

He didn't tell me what the meeting was about or who was attending. I thought to myself, *CW1 has five other staff members in his department, including CW2. Why wouldn't they send one of them?* This meant I had to ride the bus from my office to the Pentagon. I didn't want to go. I had my own work to complete.

An hour passed by, and I still didn't want to go. I attempted to find all types of excuses to avoid going. Then, I realized that nothing was working and something else was going on. I took a deep breath and thought, *This seems like a sign from God.* So, I asked God to show me another sign that I should attend. Normally, the bus ran late to get to the Pentagon; however, it was on time that day. Sign.

As I boarded the bus, a knot started forming in my stomach and I was getting nervous. During the entire bus ride, I gazed out the window asking God, "Why are you sending me to this meeting?" I arrived at the Pentagon and headed for the conference room. As I walked the halls, I asked God again, "Why are you sending me to this meeting?"

I reached the conference room 10 minutes early. As I entered the room, a young lady at the door asked, "What is your name and what agency are you with?"

I responded.

She stated, "Ok, let me see. Yes, you are the alternate for CW1. Here is your nameplate."

"Wait, what? You have me down as an alternate and I have a nameplate?" I replied.

"Yes, you were listed as an alternate for the monthly meetings, but we never saw you. We are happy to have you. Sit anywhere you please," she said.

As I sat down, I was blown away. CW1 knew I was his alternate and never told me. I was upset. Here I was in a meeting that I was supposed to be prepared for but wasn't. I hate being unprepared. *However,* I thought, *I'm not going to let them see me sweat. I will do my best. They say luck is where preparation meets opportunity. Let's see how lucky I will be.*

I sat there as others began to come in and sit down. I looked around the table at the nameplates and saw each defense agency's senior cybersecurity leader sitting there with the Department of Defense's (DoD) senior cybersecurity leader at the head of the table. As usual, I was the only woman and there were only two other black people at the table — a civilian and a colonel.

After the meeting began, the leader discussed many topics and asked questions to engage us. However, it was right before lunchtime, and many people didn't engage with him. He brought up a topic which many in the room had very little interest in; however, I had a lot of interest and experience in it. So, he and I went back and forth talking about the topic, the challenges of the topic and how we can move forward to remove the challenges from the department. Once we finished talking about that topic, the meeting ended.

As I walked out the door, the colonel approached me and said, "Hey, you seem to have the same problems we are having and I like the things you put in place at your agency. Can we talk more about it over lunch?"

I said, "Sure."

So, we went to the cafeteria and ate as we discussed his challenges.

As I was getting up to go back to my office, he stated, "Hey, I have a GS-15 position open as my deputy and chief information security officer (CISO). Your experience goes great with the challenges we are having. You should apply."

I smiled and said, "I'll think about it," then turned and walked away calmly.

As I walked away, my inner voice began to shout. I looked up at the sky and said out loud, "Really, God! Really! This is what you wanted for me?"

I couldn't believe it. I followed the signs to a new opportunity. I guess I was lucky.

The hiring process itself was a sign, not because of the position, but because of all the things that were moved for me to get the job. For example, my job interview occurred during my annual performance review for my current job, so preparation for one was preparation for both. The interviews were held in the colonel's office which was right across the hall from my boss's office; however, it just so happened that on the day of the interview, my boss was away from the office all day. It was like the Universe wanted me to have this job.

On the day of my annual performance review, my boss started the meeting by asking, "What do you want to achieve here at the agency?"

I replied, "I want to be a CISO in the next two years; however, to get there I want to be promoted to a GS-15 as the director of operations."

He said, "Why do you want to be a 15? You haven't even been a 14 an entire year yet. You aren't ready. You still need more training."

After the meeting, I thought, *During the short time he's been here, he ignored me in the halls and never took the time to get to know me nor my background. So, how can he tell me I'm not ready? He doesn't know me.* At that point, I knew he would never promote me to be a GS-15. I had no future with him nor with that agency. It was time to go.

I didn't have to wait long. Another agency thought I was ready. In November, I was promoted to a GS-15 within the Colonel's agency. In December 2014, I became a new CISO for that agency.

Memory 16: Giving in to Him

The year 2014 was unbelievable for me. I went through a hell of a lot and came out a totally different woman. As I look back on my life, I realize that even though I've been fighting God along the way, He still stood by my side to guide me. How can I deny His presence? He's shown me that with His power and my faith and works, He and I can accomplish a lot of things.

On January 1, 2015, I decided to walk into my new job and new year by giving my life over to God and getting baptized. I was reborn on February 8, 2015, and dedicated my life and time to fulfilling His purpose.

Memory 17: The Vision and Purpose

As a Christian, I took on the world with a new lens. I was healed from childhood sexual abuse and my soul was reborn. In 2015, I took every assignment and move as a step towards my purpose. I embraced every mistake and uncomfortable situation as a challenge to become a better me and find my purpose.

One day, I received an email that April was Sexual Assault Awareness Month. Hmm, I didn't know there was a month designated for sexual assault awareness. What an awesome idea! To celebrate Sexual Assault Awareness Month, the agency was hosting a panel to discuss sexual assault in the military.

As the meeting time approached, I looked at the location and thought, *That's in the Pentagon Press Room which is way on the other side of the building. I won't make it in time.* So, I made a mad dash in heels across the slippery halls of the Pentagon.

As I walked up to the door, it was closed, and the sign was blinking to not come in. So, I turned around to walk away. As I turned around, someone opened the door and said, "Come in." A sign.

I walked in and sat down to listen to the discussion, and it took me back to boot camp Cand my trigger of sexual assault training. However, as a victor, I began to engage the panel in discussions about how to best help female soldiers with sexual assault and pre-existing conditions from sexual abuse. There I was in a room with senior defense officials talking about sexual assault and how to help soldiers. Then I thought, *What about those who aren't soldiers? What about people who don't have access to these resources? What can they use?*

So, in April 2015, I made my mind up to spread the word about resources and the support services for victims and survivors of childhood sexual abuse

From April to October 2015, I volunteered to speak at engagements including women's retreats, sexual assault awareness events and high school events. During my speaking engagements, I spoke about my cyber career and life challenges and how I overcome those challenges. The speaking engagement at my hometown high school and the high school in Atlanta, Georgia, were my most memorable events.

During those presentations, I spoke to children who looked like me and came from where I came from. I spoke to them about how even though society tells you that you are supposed to live one way, life happens totally different than planned and that is ok. My educational path and career progression was provided as proof that even after being held back in first grade for not being able to read, you can still come out successful. I showed them that even though I was sexually abused as a child, I still came out successful. I demonstrated that one of my values is showing kids like them that life can suck at times, but with positive friends, relationships, resilience and dedication they can overcome anything.

After speaking at the Atlanta school, the kids came up to me and asked interesting questions like: Can a boy be sexually abused? Who can I talk to if I'm scared? Is it considered sexual abuse if it's your cousin? How do you deal with the dark moments when you want to cry? I answered their questions as the time came to an end. As I walked off the stage, a classic-dressed male teacher greeted me with a handshake and wanted to know what I did differently to heal from childhood sexual abuse.

Those types of questions guide my efforts to speak and compelled me to write this book and start a business, Hidn Trezher, LLC, to uncover the hidden treasure of your truth. I designed workshops, seminars, kits, events, and exercises to help brown girls and boys heal from childhood sexual abuse. Then, I started my new business.

DID YOU KNOW

Did you know that every state offers free resources for reporting and recovering from childhood sexual abuse? Use your search engine to search for your county and state's sexual assault resources by placing your county and state's name in the search box and add sexual assault. You will be able to locate a lot of resources that are paid through your local county taxes and donations. Please visit www.hidntrezher.org for the name, website, or phone number for other resources.

PHASE 4: REBIRTH EXERCISE

In the Rebirth Phase, you are reborn into the environment shaped by your new boundaries, standards and views. This is done through spiritual transformation, living in your truth and living a purposeful life. The goal is to build the life you want based on the new you—your boundaries, your non-negotiables, your views and your purpose.

Phase 4: Rebirth begins with deciding whether to be spiritual or not. Making the decision to be spiritual is about transforming your thoughts and actions based on a higher power for a bigger purpose than yourself. For some, the decision to spiritually change is easy. Some women can't see their lives without the connection to a higher power; however, some women are hesitant to try spiritual transformation. Let's put a pin in the Rebirth Phase for a minute.

First, I'm not here to push God, Christianity or spirituality on you. I'm here and this book is here to provide a testimony of what worked for me. Writing this didn't just happen. It took me three years to get to a point where I could write this final chapter and reshape the book for you. My writing journey was God's way of saying to me, "Cynthia, sacrifice your time and mental space to give to the body of Christ. Your mission is to serve and encourage others to grow past their hurt and pain of childhood sexual abuse to become better versions of themselves for themselves and their loved ones. Give them what I gave you."

This three-year journey resulted in my spirit guiding me to write this book for myself, then rewriting it for you. So, if you want to mark and skip the part about spiritual transformation, feel free to do so; however, spirituality was a large part of my growth in the last phase of my healing journey and it worked for me. I just ask that you try a spiritual transformation as well.

Also, before I get into the details of Phase 4, I want to be clear about a couple of hot topics related to childhood sexual abuse and spiritual transformation: the Bible as a weapon, sex in the Church, religion and sexual abuse. Each of these topics have filled hundreds of books; however, I'm not here to debate any of them. My intent is to acknowledge their impact on some people's ability to connect with a higher power and the connection itself.

Through my journey, I found three reasons why some people were turned off to religion as well as spirituality, especially the Christian faith. Reason #1 was the use of the Bible as a weapon. This reason speaks to those who use their role in the Church to oppress others, whether it is slavery or sexual abuse. Altering the Bible to manipulate or mistreat others is not of God. These issues were around since the writing and rewriting of the Bible and the expansion of the British empire, so I understand some people's hesitation.

The Bible should not be used as a weapon to beat people into submission or oppression. People who do these things are misguided Christians. Don't let them turn you away from Christianity or spirituality. I ask you to search for the right church for yourself so that you can create and grow your connection with God.

Reason #2 is the topic of sex in the Church. Now, I know for some church people, there is a stigma around talking about sex in the Church, especially to young children. But those who have that stigma should look at the topic differently. The topic of sex in the Church can be addressed from the perspective of what God gave them — reproductive organs.

I intentionally put reproductive organs, not sex. A person's sexual preference may change, but children were born with reproductive body parts that need protection. There can be a clear distinction in the discussion about the *noun* that is reproductive organs versus the *action* of sex. They are exclusive of each other. God gave us all reproductive organs and body parts.

Yes, sex is a natural act; however, the act of forcing sex is not natural and violates a person's will, including a child's will. To protect our children, we must destroy the stigma of talking about sex in the Church. Ignoring the topics of reproductive organs and sexual abuse in the Church only leaves children with one less safe place to talk to someone if they are violated. This contributes to the continuation of generational curses like childhood sexual abuse. Isn't the Church supposed to open the doors to the needs of the congregation?

Reason #3 is the topic of religion and sexual abuse. I cannot move on in the topic of religion and sexual abuse without acknowledging the topic of sexual abuse in the Church. Stories of rape in the Bible are examples of why this is an issue to be discussed in the Church. For example, Genesis 34:1-2 states when Shechem raped Dinah and 2 Samuel 13:12-14 states when Amnon raped Tamar. If people in a church ignore or suppress others who discuss sexual abuse, then that church is ignoring the needs of their congregation.

According to the United States government, child sexual abuse is a large, community health problem that can be prevented (CDC, 2021). This means that the prevention and reduction of sexual abuse takes a community of churches, teachers and friends to help children feel comfortable enough to speak to an adult as well as help victims heal and survivors overcome their unhealthy and negative barriers. To heal, we need a spiritual transformation of brown girls in adult bodies to lead the charge and open the lines of communication about sexual abuse in our communities for our communities, especially in the religious organizations.

If a church *does* take on the mission of addressing childhood sexual abuse, that church should provide time and space with a calming environment and open lines of communication for the purpose of healing, not converting. The environment should be about healing women and letting them find their own way to connect with God. Because spirituality comes from a connection with God, the healing process must start with a non-spiritual, non-religious methodical process (like mine or similar) that begins with a focus on mental health issues. Then, use joint planning procedures between a sexual assault victor and a religious leader to integrate the religion and spiritual health into the workshop. This gives a woman the information and free will that she needs to choose her relationship when she is ready. This leaves her free to grow through her trapped memories, emotions and forgiveness and not feel like she is being forced to choose a religion.

As she heals, she will freely build her religious connection based on her awareness, experiences, challenges, and satisfaction experienced from seeing it all work out but having no clue how it did. A church's role is to give the brown girls of the community the resources they need, step back, and let the higher power take it from there. She will come when she is ready. Refer to www.hidntrezher.org to request services and assistance with building a program.

So, for you that want to start your spiritual transformation, start by gathering resources from your religion of choice. Religious resources such as your Bible or Qur'an provide you with your initial set of boundaries and standards which are non-negotiables for your transformation. Next, clean out space in a closet or a small area with a door to create a worship room. Your worship room is your space to go for fighting the mental and emotional challenges of the day. Next, decorate it with your religious affirmations, resources, other positive sources of energy and a timer, but keep it simple. Finally, set aside space and time, such as in your bedtime routine, to calm yourself at night or in your morning ritual to connect or reconnect with the spirit that prepares you for your day. When you enter your worship room, set the timer for fifteen minutes to be still and listen to what inspires you.

For those who don't believe in spirituality or a higher power, find a space or a corner in your home that is big enough for you to post your positive affirmations and relax with no distractions. It will be a place where you cultivate self-care and love plus focus on your habits and responses. You can purchase small headphones or a wireless speaker to place in the room to listen to your favorite song, book or video playlist (check www.hidntrezher.org for the latest playlist of videos and songs). For new standards and boundaries, I found some personal books such as *The Secret* by Rhonda Byrne and Eckhart Tolle's *A New Earth: Awakening to Your Life's Purpose* and professional books such as *Empowering Yourself: The Organizational Game Revealed* by Harvey J. Coleman and *The 7 Habits of Highly Effective People* by Stephen Covey. These books and more as listed in the Chapter 3 and Chapter 4 Resources at the end of the book offer great perspectives on how to set non-negotiables in your life and what some of them could be.

The next step in the Rebirth Phase is to live in your truth. Living in your truth means being self-aware of your flaws and your mistakes and being ok with admitting, correcting and growing past them. Do not let your past, your mistakes or anyone define you. Let them serve as guideposts while moving forward to become a better version of you. You have come a long way and you still have a way to go. Own your journey by living in your truth and using your tools to get back on your path when you get lost.

Living your truth means accepting yourself, flaws and all, but with patience and the understanding that you are a fallible human like everyone else and that is ok. This means that as you grow, your focus should be on progression, not perfection. I encourage you to write "I'm a work in progress" on a Post-It Note, post the note on the bathroom mirror, and read it out loud three times as a part of your morning and bedtime rituals.

Life has a way of testing a person's will. As the days test your will, repeat this phrase to remind yourself that you are not perfect and are still a work in progress. If you fall back into an old habit, correct yourself by using your tools.

The next and final part of the Rebirth Phase, and this book, is living a purposeful life. Living a purposeful life means identifying your purpose for being, setting goals for yourself and moving forward in your goals.

For those of you who know your purpose, I congratulate you because many go their entire life without knowing it. For those of you who don't know your purpose, you can identify it by having patience with yourself and watching for signs and feelings of pride and completeness after you finish a task as an employee, a volunteer or a hobbyist. When you experience a sense of pride after finishing work, write down the tasks you completed, then identify the nouns and verbs of each action of your tasks. Next, search the internet for those nouns and verbs to identify the professional fields that perform those tasks. Now you have a list of fields that may be of interest to you. Finally, have patience and listen to your signs to find your purpose.

When you find that purpose, identify the steps needed to start a business to provide that service or find a company who provides it to your level of satisfaction and work for them. No matter what, take the first step to map out the process for moving towards your goal. One of my favorite activities to map out my goals for the year is a vision board party. You should try one.

As you complete this phase, I want to remind you that we are not perfect; you are not perfect. So, yes, you will experience challenges as a newbie in a new environment; however, you will get your new legs to fit this new life soon. At this point, you transformed from a survivor to a victor who can now walk in their purpose. You have the tools and armor to remain liberated from the shackles of childhood sexual abuse and you can walk with your head held high. You are on the right path to living the life you made, not one that was made by someone or something else.

EXPERIENCE AND GROWTH

When I started my rebirth phase in January 2015, I thought I was ready to take on any challenge because I thought I knew my strength and had my faith. Between the growth of my spiritual connection, living in my truth and finding my purpose, I was ready to go. I was going to kill it that year. Everything was in place to set me up for an explosive year of growth.

Yeah, no, that's not what happened. My rebirth year had lots of labor pains and choke points I had to get through. Between spousal issues, a malicious cyber-attack on my network, ageism, sexism, and racism, 2015 was a rough year. As a brown woman, "You're too young to be a GS-15" was a phrase constantly used by those at my level but older. "You're lucky to be here" were the words used in an attempt to demean my value of sitting at the table of leaders. These growth opportunities plus my thoughts, emotions, and tools ushered me through my rebirth to the other side to find my voice, my passion, and my purpose.

So, in November 2015, I decided to not only build my business but also to get my doctorate in cybersecurity. Also, I continued to take one for the team of brown girls and stay in the government until I got a sign that it was time to leave. At that point, I was healed and overflowing with resources to build the life I wanted.

LETTERS TO MY BROWN GIRLS

Brown Girls (25 and over)

Hey Ms. Lady,

I'm so proud of you. You've come a long way to get to this point. In this Rebirth Phase, you were reborn and made an environment based on your new boundaries, standards and views.

Now, I want you to get the letter that you wrote to your younger self from Phase 1. Read it out loud to yourself. How do you feel about what you said in the letter? Do you still feel the same way? Think about how much you have grown between then and now. This is your growth, not mine or anyone else's. This growth is a sign of your transition from survivor to victor.

However, one of the things I learned about being reborn is that some of your family and friends will not understand your journey or the new version of you. Some may judge you based on the environment they know you grew up in, your past unhealthy habits that served as survival tactics, plus their background and exposure to childhood sexual abuse. They will want to put you in a box that you no longer fit in. The problem is they don't know the new liberated you. They don't know your inner peace, nor do they know your purpose for being. So, you keep living in your truth and your purpose.

Today, commit yourself to being a victor and living in your own right, with your own standards and boundaries, and not allowing anything to control you. So, to appreciate your progress, take the time out to focus on what you've accomplished. Stand in front of the mirror and repeat after me:

My childhood sexual abuse no longer controls me.
I recover my life, my mind, my body and my soul.
I will keep building my standards to make this world mine.
I was a survivor, now I'm a victor.
I love me and will always value me the most.

Repeat this at least once a week to remind yourself that you are not who you used to be. Your views of the world have changed. Your boundaries and standards have changed. You are reborn as a stronger, more authentic version of yourself, and you are ready to take the world by storm. Now, go be the best version of yourself.

Love,

Another victor

Conclusion

Childhood sexual abuse is one of the most monstruous crimes committed. Not only does it impact the child when it happens, but its lasting impact is devastating to the child's growth into adulthood. When looking at the four stages of childhood sexual abuse — Innocence, Stolen Trust, Critical Attention, and Surviving — we would love to be proactive in the Innocence Stage. Once a child experiences the Stolen Trust Stage, we are reacting with an immediate race to help the child heal in the Critical Attention Stage. However, as much as we would like to react as soon as possible, it doesn't always work out that way. Most childhood sexual abuse isn't acknowledged until the Surviving Stage.

You were a survivor who decided that it was time for you heal out of the childhood sexual abuse experience. You chose the A.F.T.R. Framework to guide you through a phased approach of healing. In the Acknowledge Phase, you learned patience with yourself as you acknowledged and released trapped memories and emotions from your childhood sexual abuse. You grew patience in your natural reactions as you faced your truth as told by you. Then, you accepted forgiveness as a key part and major milestone to healing. You completed the Forgive Phase to face the emotions of anger towards people involved in your abuse for the sole purpose of releasing that anger. Forgiving yourself and others was a huge milestone for you.

Next, you transitioned from a survivor to a victor by controlling your triggers and responses. The Transition Phase taught you how to identify your unhealthy responses caused by the trauma of childhood sexual abuse, create boundaries and standards to keep your mind on a healthy path and replace your unhealthy and negative responses with healthier and positive responses. You became self-sufficient in controlling your thoughts, emotions and actions.

Finally, you built a new environment brick by brick using your new boundaries, standards and non-negotiables. These bricks of healing allowed you to be reborn into a new perspective on life and find your new truth and purpose for living. At this point, you are no longer a survivor, you are a victor. Congratulations!!!!!!!!!

You liberated yourself from trapped memories, emotions and unhealthy habits of childhood sexual abuse, and you are now reborn into a conviction of strength and pride. You should be so proud of yourself for your commitment to get through this book. I'm so proud of you, my brown girl of strength, grace, and resiliency.

Now, you can spread the word to help heal other:

- Concerned mothers who do not know how to handle their brown girl who was sexually abused,

- African American teenagers looking for a way out of an emotional spiral,

- Middle Eastern women fighting against their culture,

- Male co-workers who want to know how to talk to the sexually abused brown girl in their life.

Inform them that there are two rules to this book:
- Rule one: Have patience with yourself.

- Rule two: Healing is in the journey, not the destination.

Now, it's time for you to live your best life after healing from childhood sexual abuse. In the next thirty days, take time to practice your favorite techniques for relaxing and experiencing life. You were provided resources to help with relaxing so take them. Take the time for yourself. You've done a great job during this journey.

You traveled the path less traveled. It was my honor to serve as your companion and guide on this journey as you faced your fears and found comfort in the uncomfortable elements of liberating from your most hurtful experiences of childhood sexual abuse. You, my brown girl, embrace your journey and reset your purpose to liberate yourself beyond childhood sexual abuse.

Closure

As for me, I took one for the team and completed my goals towards my purpose and dreams. I used my healthy habits and responses to embrace my flaws and courageously became a leader in my career and the profession of cybersecurity. By doing so, I became a United States representative and global chair on a multinational and international security board of over twenty-three countries to integrate cybersecurity into military systems. In May 2018, I finished my doctorate in cybersecurity to contribute a new field of cybercrime prosecution to the field of cybersecurity. Then in June 2020, I was sworn in as a new member of the senior executive service (SES) for a United States government agency to accept my dream job as the highest cybersecurity position — a chief information security officer (CISO).

During the weeks prior to my swearing-in ceremony as an SES, I struggled to write my thank you/acceptance speech. I rewrote it six times to tell my story of how a brown girl from the projects navigated to become an SES in seven years instead of the average twenty-three years and join the ranks of the 1 percent of black women in the SES corp. I was so excited to do what I love for this new agency.

As many times as I rewrote my speech, it never felt right. The night before my ceremony, it hit me. The message I had wasn't for the audience that was watching my ceremony. My message was for my brown girls looking for inspiration, motivation and guidance on how to navigate around barriers in life such as the ones that come from childhood sexual abuse. So, I rewrote my speech thanking my family and showing my appreciation for the leaders of the agency.

Since my swearing-in ceremony, I've been living my dream of speaking to women and children about childhood sexual abuse. I have also been mentoring numerous women and men through their careers and being mentored by some great brown women. It has all been so fulfilling and I am enjoying every minute of it. I've been blessed to heal and live my dreams and I hope you will as well.

I'm glad you chose to purchase this book to serve as your companion as you go along your journey. I look forward to hearing your stories about how you acknowledged your truth, forgave your past, transitioned to a new future and are living your life reborn as the best version of yourself.

Now, join me in listening to Ledisi's *If You Don't Mind*. This song gives me life.

Letter to My Support System

Liberation using the A.F.T.R. Framework helped me realize that throughout my life there were beacons of light that pulled me out of my darkness in moments when things could have easily gone the other way. From 1992 to 2005, many of you were unaware that I was in survival mode. I was trying to figure out how to keep my mental health together and not fall apart as a survivor. Now, I live my life as a victor. But, Lord knows, I couldn't have done it without you guys.

This book is a testimony of my journey to heal from childhood sexual abuse. I acknowledge those who were a blessing to my survival, my transition and my healing from being a scared, shy brown girl to a strong brown woman. This book was not possible without the two people who I could call on as dedicated sources of positive energy:

- Marcus Littlejohn: My best friend. Since the eighth grade, you were there when I had no one to talk to. You were the friend that I needed and the first male I was able to trust. I know I've laid a lot on you throughout these years, but you took it all on as a brother does. You were there with that infectious laugh, bright smile, kind heart, emotional support and love I needed. Thanks for 30 years of friendship. I wouldn't be here without you. Love you, Bruh.

- Elnora Littlejohn (Late): I can't say enough about you. As a teenager, there were days where I didn't know where to turn. You helped me through my emotions, and you helped me to understand forgiveness. Your loving embrace during my bouts of tears engulfed me with so much motherly love that I wanted to be a better person for you. When you passed away in May 2012, I cried. To this day, I still cry. There are days I still miss you, but I know you watch over me. Your spirit still motivates me to be the best version of myself.

To my friends who didn't know all of this, when you read this book you are going to ask, "Why didn't you tell me? I thought we were friends." I was embarrassed and made every attempt to avoid dealing with it. Your homes, your parents and you helped me stay sane through it all. Much love to each of you for the laughter, the clubbing, the parties and just everything. I can't thank all of you, but I have to acknowledge:

- My favorite twins: Drienna and Dominque. Thanks for the support, love and sharing your parents with me. Your mom and dad held no cut cards on parental advice, and I love them ever more for it. They were what I needed. Thanks Ma Pon and Jake (RIH).

- Dr. Michelle Harris: Your belief in this book has been what I needed to get it done. Thanks for being my accountability partner, a soror (OO-OOOP) and my sister in Christ. Thank you for the last twenty-five years of friendship.

- My Gaffney Girls: Kimberly Gaffney-Charles and Dr. Alexea Gaffney. Your love and commitment to whatever I am doing never ceases to amaze me. As partners in motherhood, Peloton, marriage and life, you ladies have been my true ride or die for twenty-five years. Thanks for the babysitting services, emotional and mental support, years of friendship and sisterhood.

Finally, to my mom and dad: The year 2014 was a major year for our relationship. The lesson I learned was that parents try their best with what they know and what they have. I appreciate the love and support you guys have given me during my growth. Our past is just that — our past. It allowed us to grow. Now, it's only up from here with us. I love you guys.

God blessed me with some special friends and family. I can't thank you all, but you each played a significant role in my life.

Healing cannot be done without a support system. Whether it is your family or friends, I advise you, the victor, to choose people who will hold you accountable and be positive sources of energy as you take your journey to heal.

Resources

Women who were sexually abused as children and left with limited access to healing resources react in unhealthy ways such as turning to alcohol, drugs, self-mutilation or suicide. Some will do almost anything to take themselves away from the emotions and stress triggered by the memories of childhood sexual abuse. These resources are listed as mechanisms for a survivor to heal in private or in public.

Chapter 1 Resources

Amigos for Kids. (2021). *Awareness is Key*. Child Abuse Gallery. Retrieved from https://amigosforkids.org/awareness

Broken Crayons. (2021). *Sometimes, A Child's Drawings Can Paint a Much Bigger Picture*. Retrieved from https://brokencrayons.us/

Center for Disease Control. (2021). *Preventing Child Sexual Abuse*. Retrieved from https://www.cdc.gov/violenceprevention/childabuseandneglect/childsexualabuse.html

Childhelp. (2021). *Childhelp National Child Abuse Hotline*. Phone: 1-800-4-A-Child. Retrieved from https://www.childhelp.org

Darkness 2 Light. (2021). *End Child Sexual Abuse.* Phone: 1-866-FOR-LIGHT (866-367-5444). Retrieved from https://www.d2l.org/resources/

King, K., & King, Z. (2020). *I Said No: A Kid-To-Kid Guide to Keeping Private Parts Private.* Retrieved from https://isaidno.info

National Center for Missing and Exploited Children. (2021). Retrieved from https://www.missingkids.org/Home

National Sexual Violence Resource Center. (2021). *Preventing Child Sexual Abuse Resources.* Retrieved from https://www.nsvrc.org/preventing-child-sexual-abuse-resources

Parenting Safe Children. (2021). *Keeping Children Safe from Sexual Assault — In Your Community.* Retrieved from https://parentingsafechildren.com/

RAINN (Rape, Abuse & Incest National Network). (2021). *I'm a Kid and Something Happened.* Retrieved from https://rainn.org/articles/i-am-kid-and-something-happened

Stop Abuse. (2021). Retrieved from https://stopabuse.com

U.S. Department of Health & Human Services. (2021). *Child Welfare Information Gateway.* Retrieved from https://www.childwelfare.gov/

U.S. Department of Health & Human Services. (2021). *Children's Bureau*. Retrieved from https://www.acf.hhs.gov/cb

Chapter 2 Resources

Meditation Activities/Apps:

- Calm.com (2021)

- Peloton app has meditation and yoga.

- RAINN app has hotline and self-care. Learn and find help near you.

Healing Therapy for Stress and Anger: Search your area for these types of resources.

- Martial Arts and Self-Defense Class

- Dance Therapy Sessions at your local dance studio

- Art Therapy Sessions at your local library or college

Chapter 3 Resources

Replacements for unhealthy habits include:

- Yoga classes from YouTube or your local gym can provide alternatives to unhealthy habits.

- YouTube: Build a YouTube playlist using similar resources as above that positively feeds your thoughts.

Chapter 4 Resources

Here are some life-altering books I love reading and have read at least four times each:

- Coelho, Paulo. (1994). *The Alchemist.*
- Coleman, Harvey J. (2010). *Rules of the Game for Life, College, High School.*
- Dr. Seuss Enterprises. (1990). *Oh, The Places You'll Go!*

Check www.hidntrezher.org for the latest websites, apps and resources.

References

Barnett, B. (2016). *What is the Age of Consent in the United States?* Retrieved from https://www.bhwlawfirm.com/legal-age-consent-united-states-map

Center for Disease Control and Prevention. (2021). *Preventing Child Sexual Abuse.* Retrieved from https://www.cdc.gov/violenceprevention/childabuseandneglect/childsexualabuse.html

National Congress of American Indians. (2021). *Tribal Nations & the United States: An Introduction.* Retrieved from https://ncai.org/about-tribes

Oludare, A. (2015). *Cybercrime Prevention and Law Enforcement: A Comparative Analysis of Nigeria and the United States of America.* Retrieved from ProQuest: 10100954

US Code Title 18, Section 2243. (2022). *Sexual Abuse of a Minor or Ward.* Retrieved from https://govinfo.gov/content/pkg/USCODE-2011-title18/html/USCODE-2011-title18-partI-chap109A.htm

Thomas, S., Bannister, S., Hall, J. (2011). *Anger in the Trajectory of Healing from Childhood Maltreatment.* Retrieved from https://www.ncbi.nlm.nih.gov/pmc/articles/PMC3361676/#__ffn_sectitle

UNICEF. (2021). *Child Rights and Human Rights Explained*. Retrieved from https://unicef.org/child-rights-convention/children-human-rights-explained

Appendices

Appendix A: Acknowledgment Phase - Release Memory

_____
_____
_____
_____
_____
_____
_____
_____
_____
_____
_____
_____
_____
_____
_____
_____
_____
_____
_____
_____
_____
_____

Appendix B: Acknowledge Resource – Dear Anger Letter

_____

_____

_____

_____

_____

_____

_____

_____

_____

_____

_____

_____

_____

_____

_____

_____

_____

_____

_____

_____

_____

_____

_____

_____

Appendix C: Acknowledge Resource - Letter to You

Dear _____

_____

_____

_____

_____

_____

_____

_____

_____

_____

_____

_____

_____

_____

_____

_____

_____

_____

_____

_____

_____

_____

_____

_____

Dr. Cynthia Sutherland

Appendix D: Forgive Resource - Letter to You

_____

_____

_____

_____

_____

_____

_____

_____

_____

_____

_____

_____

_____

_____

_____

_____

_____

_____

_____

_____

_____

_____

_____

_____

_____

Appendix E: Forgiving Resource - Letter to Your Abuser

_____

_____

_____

_____

_____

_____

_____

_____

_____

_____

_____

_____

_____

_____

_____

_____

_____

_____

_____

_____

_____

_____

_____

_____

Appendix F: Transition Phase – Habit Table (Example)

Date	Trigger	Response	Outputs
11/10/2016	Unexpected or late bill caused you to feel stress.	Ignore bill OR pay bill late even though you have the money and time to pay it. Don't create a budget or an emergency fund.	Prolonged stress and anxiety.

For more space, visit www.drcys.com
to purchase a habit journal.

About the Author

Cynthia Sutherland, D.Sc. is a sexual abuse victor, public speaker, and author who overcame mental health obstacles to become a decorated Army veteran, award-winning national and global cybersecurity leader, and Doctor in Cybersecurity. During her career climb, Dr.CyS® created a safe space for awareness and holistic healing of childhood sexual abuse survivors as they grow in their profession.

Through her company, HIDN Trezher, a nonprofit organization, Cynthia Sutherland, D.Sc. offers private and public support services, sexual assault awareness events, and more. Her group services include program development for community and religious organizations, a "Give Me Your Hand" workshop, and "Permission to Heal" seminar.

Cynthia Sutherland, D.Sc.'s purpose in life is to provide a lifeline of resources to educate, heal, and empower survivors of childhood sexual abuse. She is also building a global support movement and symbol of hope for survivors.

Dr. Cynthia lives in the Washington, D.C., area with her family.

Learn more at www.drcys.com

CREATING DISTINCTIVE BOOKS
WITH INTENTIONAL RESULTS

We're a collaborative group of creative masterminds
with a mission to produce high-quality books to position
you for monumental success in the marketplace.

Our professional team of writers, editors, designers,
and marketing strategists work closely together to ensure
that every detail of your book is a clear representation
of the message in your writing.

Want to know more?
Write to us at info@publishyourgift.com
or call (888) 949-6228

Discover great books, exclusive offers, and more at
www.PublishYourGift.com

Connect with us on social media

@publishyourgift